Square Peg

Also by Katherine Ellison

Buzz: A Year of Paying Attention

The Mommy Brain:
How Motherhood Makes You Smarter

The New Economy of Nature:
The Quest to Make Conservation Profitable

And

Imelda: Steel Butterfly of the Philippines

Square Peg

MY STORY AND WHAT IT MEANS
FOR RAISING INNOVATORS, VISIONARIES,
AND OUT-OF-THE-BOX THINKERS

L. Todd Rose

· WITH ·

Katherine Ellison

HYPERION

NEW YORK

Library of Congress Cataloging-in-Publication Data has been applied for.

ISBN: 978-1-4013-2427-8

Book design by Victoria Hartman

FIRST EDITION

10   9   8   7   6   5   4   3   2   1

THIS LABEL APPLIES TO TEXT STOCK

We try to produce the most beautiful books possible, and we are also extremely
concerned about the impact of our manufacturing process on the forests of the world
and the environment as a whole. Accordingly, we've made sure that all of the paper
we use has been certified as coming from forests that are managed, to ensure the
protection of the people and wildlife dependent upon them.

For Lyda, Ruth, and Bernice.
Heroines.

● ■ ●

"This important book shows how people learn and develop differently, with diverse values, goals, and commitments. We naturally learn in different ways for various reasons. There is no single pathway to learning that everyone follows, but instead variable ways of learning based on diverse goals and values. This analysis of education should be the starting point of teaching and learning, the groundwork of pedagogy from top to bottom. The book lays out the framework for a new kind of education, grounded in the individual, not the fiction of one common learning pathway. Only with this new framework will schools recognize and celebrate the differences that make students unique. Only then will teaching and learning help all children to reach their potential. This must be the starting point of the new framework for education."

— KURT W. FISCHER

Director of the Mind, Brain, and Education Institute
Harvard Graduate School of Education

Contents

Prologue: Surrendering the Rain Sticks   1

1 · My Bright Future   21

2 · Smart Criminal   41

3 · Why Context Matters   65

4 · Ostracized   85

5 · Fitting In—and Dropping Out   107

6 · Social Justice   128

7 · Turnaround   148

8 · Failing Well   172

Epilogue: Creating New Contexts for Learning   198

Acknowledgments   219

Notes   223

Bibliography   239

Square Peg

Surrendering the Rain Sticks

"The difficulty lies, not in the new ideas, but in escaping from the old ones. . . ."

—JOHN MAYNARD KEYNES

Seventh-Grade Satan

It's said that you can tell when the Devil is near by the smell of burning sulfur. And while my seventh-grade art teacher, Mr. Peabody, may not have believed this, literally, I wouldn't be surprised to hear the thought crossed his mind on the afternoon I threw a makeshift stink bomb—well, actually six stink bombs—at his blackboard.

In the twenty-two years that have passed since that time, I've sometimes thought back on my diabolical naughtiness as a justified protest against the way he taught us—always talking about art, but never having us do anything. A rail-thin man with sunken eyes, he mumbled a lot and seemed to be counting down the days to his retirement. Perhaps my defiance should be considered as a noble act of civil disobedience: my eloquent rebellion against a broken system.

Or maybe not. A few minutes earlier, my friend Ryan had dared me to do it—and I've always been a sucker for dares.

The bomb was made of six small vials of ammonium sulfide, a mixture beloved by generations of pranksters for its powerful stench of rotten eggs. Ryan had handed the vials to me moments earlier, suggesting I walk to the back of the room as if to sharpen my pencil, and throw them while Mr. Peabody stood at the blackboard with his back turned to the class.

Looking back, I suppose it's no surprise that things turned out so much worse than I'd expected. First, I really should have taken a few seconds to think before I acted, during which I might have realized that there was no way I could have avoided getting caught—and punished. Second, Ryan no doubt should have told me he'd meant for me to throw just one vial, not all six.

Oh well!

The funny thing is that at the moment I hurled those vials at the blackboard, I was just as surprised as the other students by the loud noise of the shattering glass, and by how thoroughly the air filled with the stink. The smoke brought tears to our eyes and obliged Mr. Peabody to usher us all out of the classroom. Once he had us lined up against the wall outside, it didn't take a great detective to zero in on the culprit; while every other student was crying and choking on the synthetic fart fumes, I was the only one laughing.

My teacher grabbed me by the back of my neck, like a dog, and marched me to the principal's office—by then familiar territory—where I was "detained" for an hour until my mother, fuming quite a bit herself, arrived to pick me up. I was suspended from school—yet again—for the rest of the week.

My Two Futures

The stink bomb was my worst offense that year, and one more black mark on a growing record that vexed both my teachers and my bewildered parents. By the age of thirteen, I was already (and seemingly permanently) labeled as a troublemaker. I was the kid who makes other students laugh during class, but whom no one sits next to at lunch; the kid who'd failed so many times by then that he'd rather get an F on an assignment than admit he didn't understand the lesson; the kid who attracted detentions and demerits more often than praise and rewards. In short, I was the square peg in the round hole of our local school system.

It wouldn't have surprised anyone who knew me back then if I'd landed in jail by my twenties. It did surprise just about everyone that I wound up on the faculty of Harvard University.

Looking back, I know there was no single intervention that turned my life around. No heart-to-heart talk with a great teacher. No perfectly tailored drug that helped me sit still and concentrate. I wasn't "scared straight" by a probation officer. My parents never found a magic guide to raising me right. I didn't wake up one morning and suddenly turn over a new leaf.

Instead, my future emerged from a series of at first seemingly random, yet always interrelated, circumstances and events. These include, but weren't limited to: my father's professional promotion, which allowed us to move to a new town just when I needed a second chance; the patience of a socially skilled football player whom I decided to emulate; and a spring afternoon when I impulsively stole a textbook from a lovely high school senior. I can't say for certain how my life would have played out in the absence of any of these or several other experiences. I simply know that I always had within me the raw materials for what anyone might suppose are two mirror-opposite paths: leading either to prison or to Harvard.

I eventually found my way to the more prestigious destination, and today I have the honor of collaborating with some of the nation's brightest scientists and entrepreneurs on delightfully challenging problems. Through it all, I can't help but marvel at how little I, myself, have changed, even as the way I'm perceived has been transformed by this new set of circumstances. In my Ivy League enclave, my high school impertinence is seen as wit. What used to be my lack of respect for authority is now viewed as iconoclastic insight. My lack of inhibition is now interpreted as creativity.

Twenty-two years ago, however, as the noxious fumes filled that art class, most people who knew me weren't so much admiring as perplexed or even appalled. Why on earth, after an intelligence test I'd taken before starting kindergarten showed that I was unusually smart, was I doing so many stupid things? Why was I so intent on sabotaging myself? Why did I seem destined for a life of self-inflicted failure while others, seemingly less gifted, succeeded?

These questions have weighed on my mind continually ever since the joyful day (for both me and my hapless teachers) that I left Sand Ridge Junior High School. And I'm not alone in asking them.

Over the past several decades, researchers and policy makers have dedicated careers to trying to understand what makes kids like me tick—and how on earth to make us tick more quietly.

The trouble isn't a lack of opinions. I've heard my behavior ascribed to everything from sheer diabolical nature, to laziness, to a cry for help, to an excess of TV, to having a brain deficiency— a reference to the fact that the same year I threw the stink bombs, I was diagnosed with attention deficit/hyperactivity disorder, or ADHD.

None of these all-over-the-map hypotheses caused me near the frustration, however, as I felt on one particular afternoon in Utah, in the year 2000, roughly twelve years after the stink-bomb affair. An anguished mother, having read a newspaper story about my unlikely comeback and recent acceptance to graduate school at Harvard, visited me at my in-laws' house. She figured I'd have insights in how to deal with her own struggling son. He, too, had been diagnosed with ADHD and was failing academically and rebelling in school.

As I listened to her tale, I could see that she'd done everything she could think of to help her son. She'd escorted him to medical experts, secured a diagnosis and prescription for stimulant drugs, and fought for accommodations for him at school. Yet he was still on the skids: feeling miserable, and causing misery to everyone who cared about him.

By then, this mother had come to the sad realization that doctors could only do so much for her child, and that something more was needed. She was looking to me for the answers, and at that point I'm pretty sure she would have signed up her son for round-the-clock tap-dancing lessons, or a diet of pure wheatgrass, if I had told her such methods had worked for me. As much as I wanted to help, however, I had nothing useful to say. The truth was that I really didn't understand how I'd turned my life around. I'll never forget the look in her eyes when I told her as much, or how she left the house in tears.

The encounter so humbled me that I vowed I would wait to talk about my story in public only when I felt sure I could offer something useful for parents in similar predicaments.

A decade has passed, and today, at last, I have something to say.

It's Complex . . .

At eighteen years old, I was a failure: a high school dropout stocking shelves at a department store for $4.25 an hour. Sixteen years later, I was a success: a young faculty member at the Harvard Graduate School of Education. As I've mentioned, there's no easy explanation for my turnaround, and, frankly, I've yet to find much enlightenment from either conventional psychology or mainstream theories of education. Instead, I'm convinced that the most valuable insights derive from a new scientific field known as *complex systems*.

To put it simply, the study of complex systems looks at how different parts of a system influence each other collectively to produce various outcomes. Nowadays, scientists have been holding up this lens to a range of traditional disciplines, from physics to biology—and, most recently, in centers like the one in which

I work: Harvard's Mind, Brain, and Education program—to the study of human learning. As this effort matures, it is offering a radically new and useful way for parents and teachers to understand the often bewildering behavior of children in their charge.

No matter whether your subject is an A student or a stink-bomb-throwing rebel, the perspective of complex systems will help you see that an individual's behavior at any given time will depend on much more than that person's genetic code or even his or her best efforts. Instead, *all* behavior emerges from the constant interaction between a person's biology, past experiences, and the immediate environment, or context. These interactions happen through what scientists call feedback loops—powerful mechanisms that, if left unchecked, can kick-start a cascade of actions and reactions, in which small differences end up having an enormous impact on the outcomes.

Feedback loops are what explains the famous "butterfly effect"—the idea, first proposed by the mathematician and climatologist Edward Lorenz in the 1960s (and, incidentally, the title of a so-so movie starring Ashton Kutcher), that a butterfly flapping its wings in Brazil can set off a tornado in Texas.

...But You Don't Need Any Math

Through the rest of this book, I'll elaborate on four ideas derived both from the study of complex systems and recent neuroscience findings, which I believe can help make you a much more understanding and effective parent and teacher. Here they are, in brief:

1. Variability is the rule: As humans, our ways of perceiving the world and reacting to what we perceive are much more diverse and dynamic than we might ever have imagined.
2. Emotions are serious stuff: Contrary to what we've long believed, modern neuroscience has shown that there is no such thing as purely rational thought or behavior. Parents and teachers need to learn to tune in to children's emotional states to help them make the most of their education.
3. Context is key: People often behave in dramatically different ways, depending on the circumstances. Among other things, this suggests that we unfairly prejudice children by labeling them with a disorder, when they'd be perfectly fine in a different environment.
4. Feedback loops determine long-term success or failure: Remember those flapping butterfly wings, and keep in mind that small changes in your child's life today can make an enormous difference tomorrow.

Once you start reflecting on how behavior can be shaped, moment to moment, by interactions between your child and his or her context, complex systems may seem like a no-brainer. Little Johnny, a bitter pill at home with his kid brother, is a sweetheart at his friend's house. Alternatively, your moody teenager calls you an "idiot" and your explosive reaction has less to do with that choice of words than your memory of a fight you had with your own dad in 1973 and the fact that you slept less than six hours the night before.

In fact, if you've ever watched a baseball game, you already intuitively understand how complex systems work. Why is it that a big-league pitcher can't throw the same curveball every time? Despite his exceptional skill, and thousands of hours of practice, his performance with any given pitch will depend on a variety of contextual factors that mostly are beyond his control: the wind velocity, the cheering or booing from the stands, whether or not there is a runner on base, and even his perception of his competitors' skill, all play their parts.

So do feedback loops. Imagine the same pitcher in the middle of a meltdown. He's been doing just fine for six innings until, out of the blue, he throws a bad pitch, and then another, and another. Suddenly the bases are loaded; the crowd is jeering, and while the pitcher is trying to keep his mind on the next pitch, he also has an eye on the dugout—will the manager pull him out soon? Adrenaline surges through his bloodstream. His heart beats faster; he's sweating, and his hands are starting to shake. Not surprisingly, the next pitch is way off the mark, and he is yanked from the game.

With curveballs, as with stink bombs, the same rule applies. Behavior isn't something someone "has." Rather, it emerges from the interaction of a person's biology, past experiences, and immediate context.

Surrendering the Rain Sticks

If all this is starting to seem pretty obvious, let me offer a suggestion as to why so many of us—unfortunately including so many school administrators—continue to resist the wisdom of complex systems. It boils down to one of the most basic human needs, which is to believe that we have total control over our fates. The history of philosophy, on top of every individual's life experience, tells us otherwise, and still we poignantly persist.

It's a lot like the way societies have clung to the belief, since ancient times, that we can make it rain. Mexico's Mayans resorted to fearsome human sacrifices, while Native Americans used chants and rain sticks. Today we trust in meteorologists, who use powerful computers and sophisticated mathematical algorithms yet, even so, are often as surprised as the rest of us by sudden storms and heat waves.

The difficulty is that the weather will always depend on an assortment of constantly fluctuating influences. And to be sure, we've made progress in accepting this rule—when it comes to the weather. We've surrendered the sacrifices and chants and sticks as tools to make it rain. Yet when it comes to our kids, we're still seeking that magic bullet. Today, a multibillion-dollar industry of pharmaceuticals, dietary supplements, computerized training programs, and other interventions sustains the illusion that as parents and teachers we can "fix" a child's behavior and save him or her from failure. The reality is that we can't, for the simple reason that behavior, like the weather, is staggeringly complex.

That's why our first step must be, finally, to put down those rain sticks when it comes to our kids, and shift over to the complex-systems view of behavior. We must do this in our homes, but more importantly also in our schools, where our children, after all, spend most of their waking hours.

My hope with this book is to give you several more insights into how this can happen, based on what I've learned both from my own fall-and-rise journey and the gradual and quite hopeful transformations I've been witnessing at many schools throughout this country. Before I leave the story of those stink bombs aside, however, I want to offer you one more clue to the context of my rebellion. It was an incident that took place in another class, several months earlier, and is unfortunately the kind of small but potentially devastating event that clouds all too many a square peg's future.

No Chocolate for Me

Here's how it went down: My English teacher, whom I'll call Mr. Meany (since I'm being completely objective here), had offered a giant Snickers bar to the student who wrote the best poem. Unlike Mr. Peabody, Mr. Meany was one of the more popular teachers at Sand Ridge Junior High. He coached a recreational basketball team and even occasionally took some of us kids on ski trips. I wanted him to like me and felt this was my big chance. I'd been writing poetry for years, filling up notebooks I occasionally showed to my mother and grandmother. The two of them had encouraged me so much that I was sure I'd have an easy chance to win that Snickers bar.

So, in a big departure from what by then was my normal homework MO (that is, to ignore it), I labored at the kitchen table for several evenings straight. By the end, I'd come up with a full-page, lyrical ode to ski jumping.

Here's how it began, complete with my primitive spelling:

My eyes are courageous
But my heart fears fate
My legs are like steal [sic]
As I approached [sic] *the gate . . .*

To this day, I remember the look my parents gave me as they watched their oldest son finally taking school seriously. Dared they hope for a turning point?

I turned the poem in on time, and even bragged to other kids in the class that I was sure I was going to win. But when the teacher handed back the poems a few days later, not only had I not won the chocolate bar, but he'd given me an F.

It took me a few seconds to register the meaning of the big red letter scrawled on my poem, but as soon as I did, I jumped out of my chair and stalked up to Mr. Meany, who was by then back at his desk.

"Hey, why'd I get an F?" I demanded, not even trying to use my indoor voice.

Mr. Meany looked at me as if he were disappointed that I hadn't figured it out.

"You couldn't have written this," he said.

I felt like my head was about to explode. "Of course I wrote this. I worked on this for three nights," I said. "You can ask my mom!"

Mr. Meany just shook his head and ordered me back to my seat. The next day, my mother came to school to argue on my behalf, confirming that she had watched me write the poem and offering to bring in other poems that I had written. Yet my teacher still refused to change my grade. As I walked out of the school with my furious mother, I remember thinking, "I quit. I really, really quit." Until then, I'd been told so often that my failures were caused by my lack of trying. But now I had tried—and I'd been robbed.

Like all of the subsequent events I'll be relating, this story isn't as simple as it may at first sound. On his good days, Mr. Meany was not mean at all. Still, he was managing a crowded class with several difficult characters aside from myself, and he already had good reason to doubt my sincerity. After all, this was the first sign he'd seen that I might care about school in any way, and maybe what I cared most about was the chocolate.

I want to be clear: I'm not arguing that my loss of the Snickers bar justified my throwing those stink bombs. It obviously did not. Still, I've often wondered how my middle school career might have progressed if Mr. Meany had believed I'd written that poem. Maybe he would have encouraged me to show him more of the work I'd been hiding until then. Maybe I would have started to think of myself as a writer, instead of a screw-up. The flap of a butterfly's wings in my English class might in this way have led to a completely different kind of tornado than those stink bombs in the art class.

Instead, however, the incident tipped the scales that were already loaded with hundreds of less dramatic mishaps shaping how I saw the world and myself. From that point on, I made good on my silent vow to stop trying. My parents, struggling to raise five kids while my dad worked all day and went to school at night, cajoled, bribed, and threatened me, mostly in vain, for four more years, as I determinedly wasted everyone's time right up until the middle of my senior year in high school. That's when my principal informed them that, given my GPA—an appalling 0.9—there was no way I'd graduate. And so, at eighteen, I dropped out of high school.

The Million-Dropout March

In flunking out, I not only dashed my poor parents' hopes, but joined a modern American trend that retired General Colin Powell has dubbed a "moral catastrophe."

At this writing, more than a quarter of U.S. high school students—1.2 million at last count—drop out every year. That's roughly seven thousand students a day—a day!—making our shameful rate one of the highest in the industrialized world.

The cost to these students (and their families) is enormous, as dropping out of high school is one of the surest predictors of lifelong failure.

To be sure, we've all heard legends about the smart, quirky dropouts who went on to professional glory, among them the beloved author Mark Twain (Samuel Clemens), the famed photographer Ansel Adams, the billionaire businessman Richard Branson, and the former British prime minister John Major. Yet I look at this phenomenon as a glass that is tragically half-empty. When I consider the tremendous contributions that these hardy survivors made to society, I can't help but calculate that for every George Gershwin (the famed composer) there are in all probability thousands, if not millions of other bright young dropouts who simply have lacked the resilience or resources or lucky breaks needed to turn their lives around. Their talents are forever lost to us.

America's dropout crisis, in other words, is not only a problem for individuals and families—it's a drag on all of us. The cost amounts not only from the value of all that lost potential but also from the expense of taking care of lives ruined in the process. Most students who quit school early end up in dead-end jobs, earning much less than their peers, or land in prison. One study found that more than 80 percent of U.S. prison inmates were dropouts. Another pegged the cost of America's yearly dropouts, mostly in terms of crime and unemployment programs, at more than $240 billion a year.

My own story varies from the standard dropout tale. The vast majority of American youth who quit school are chronic low-achievers, and many come from low-income families. In contrast, I belonged to the relative minority of dropouts from hardworking, emerging middle-class families with a fervent belief in the value of education and with high expectations for their children. Moreover, as I've mentioned, when I started out in school, tests showed that I had the smarts to succeed. But along the way, things started going wrong, with a momentum that built until it seemed there was no going back.

While, again, my story isn't average, its broad outlines are more common than you might suppose. For one thing, as many as one-third of America's dropouts have learning differences that in the context of traditional schools are serious enough to result in medical diagnoses (an issue I'll return to later in these pages), while as many as 5 percent of all high school dropouts are intellectually gifted. What this means is that tens of thousands of bright students a year end up giving up and failing out of a system that failed them first.

Granted, students like I used to be aren't the easiest to teach. Yet I'd argue this says more about the state of modern classrooms than it does about us. Did I say modern? The conventions prevailing today in most schools throughout the world, in which rote memorization is still, anachronistically, prized originated in early-nineteenth-century Prussia, where the compulsory school system was designed to churn out loyal and obedient soldiers and factory workers. The model was never meant to nurture individual potential or creativity, but rather to instill uniformity and compliance. This view of education is directly at odds with the foundational ideas of the United States of America, and it is woefully obsolete in an era where more jobs demand a high level of autonomy and the skill to manage a never-ending flood of information.

Moreover, our current educational system is in fact all but unequipped to cope with what neuroscience has revealed as the extraordinary variability in the way children learn, and the powerful role that context plays in shaping outcomes. Kurt Fischer, my mentor and colleague at Harvard, where he is the director of Harvard University's Mind, Brain, and Education program, goes so far as to say that today's schools essentially fail about 80 percent of students. Sure, kids get through. Yet simply surviving is not a high enough bar for our educational system—not by a long shot. Worse still, our schools are often downright damaging in the long term for children who by temperament are prone to question authority—the kinds of kids who can't help but think differently, who like to take risks, and who represent America's best hope to innovate its way to a better future.

Unfortunately, instead of focusing on changing an obviously broken educational context, we have to date largely put the blame on our hardworking teachers—and perhaps even more so on our children, millions of whom are themselves treated as broken because our system cannot deal with natural learning variability. At last count, more than 5.4 million U.S. children had been diagnosed with ADHD, while millions more are coping with one or more of a variety of other diagnoses, from dyslexia to dyscalculia (trouble with math), to dysgraphia (difficulty writing), and so on. Most of these kids slog through years of school, during which they're disengaged at best, and disruptive or delinquent at worst. Researchers report that up to 60 percent of children with ADHD will be suspended in high school, and as many as 36 percent will drop out. Nor is it any secret that U.S. prisons are crowded with grown-up versions of youth who don't fit in. By some estimates as many as half of all U.S. prison inmates meet the criteria for a learning disability.

The good news is that it doesn't have to be this way—and I'm convinced that it won't be for much longer. In fact, as I'll show you, we're now at the start of what I see as a once-in-a-lifetime opportunity to transform the educational environment through a careful integration of technologies and advances from the modern learning sciences. At this writing, pioneering schools throughout the United States are already starting to adopt new approaches to teaching based on cutting-edge scientific advances in learning. They're rejecting rigid, tried-and-failed approaches, such as memorization and standardized tests, in favor of dynamic, flexible, personalized, and adaptive solutions that actually support the natural differences children bring to school with them. Many of these efforts are inspired by the struggles of kids like I used to be, who've long been on the margins of our teach-to-the-middle traditions. Yet what's particularly exciting about these new approaches is that their promise extends well beyond square pegs to include *all* students—making learning more engaging, and igniting creativity.

Of course all the technology in the world will never be enough, by itself, to solve the problem. There is much that you can do, as I intend to show you, to make the most of this historic opportunity. That's why this book is both a memoir and a manifesto. I'm sharing my story in the hopes of helping parents and teachers help kids at home and at school. Yet more broadly, it's high time to demand that our schools finally catch up to what scientists (and good teachers) have known for years about the most effective ways to learn and teach. We need nothing less than a learning revolution to stop that next stink bomb in midair—and save the troublemaking square peg with the glass vials in his hand for more creative and healthy pursuits.

As you read along, I hope you'll see what I mean. And please don't worry about taking notes. At the end of each chapter, I'll offer a summary of the "big ideas" from complex systems, plus related action items you can use to support the square pegs in your own lives.

It works like this:

BIG IDEAS
● ■ ■ ■ ● ■ ● ■ ●

- You can make a really cool stink bomb by mixing hydrogen sulfide and ammonium.

- Parents can do much more to influence your children's future than you may now believe; just not in the way you might believe.

- Four concepts from neuroscience and complex systems can help you better understand and support your child:
  - Human brains are surprisingly variable.
  - Emotion is a much more powerful influence on behavior—and particularly on learning—than we have previously thought.
  - Behavior can't be understood independent of its context.
  - Feedback loops are a powerful mechanism through which biology and context interact and reinforce each other. You can't control them, but with some understanding, you may influence them.

- America has one of the industrialized world's highest annual rates of high school dropouts, thousands of whom are intellectually gifted.

- A fledgling revolution in the learning sciences, based on the same complex-systems ideas presented in this book, promises to transform education and (in the process) re-chart the life course of many a smart square peg, and to make school more effective for millions of other children.

ACTION ITEMS
• ■ • ■ ■ • ■ • ■ • ■ •

- Keep reading.
- Hug your kid.
- Start today to look at your world, and particularly your child's behavior, through the lens of complex systems, keeping in mind the four key concepts of variability, emotion, context, and feedback loops.

My Bright Future

"Context is the key—from that comes the understanding
of everything."

—Kenneth Noland

"He's Yours Now!"

On my first morning of kindergarten, my mother, a trim blond woman with bright blue eyes that rarely conceal her emotions, looked around at all the other moms dropping off their kids at the school door and was struck by the fact that she alone was smiling.

"He's yours now!" were her first words to my new teacher.

Can I blame her? At five years old, I was the eldest of her three children—there would be five in all, eventually—and, as she had soon realized, *this wasn't what most kids were like.*

I had begun making trouble from my first night home from the hospital. Not once throughout my first two years had I slept through the night, a torturous habit, for my parents, that I compounded as soon as I outgrew my crib, by sleepwalking, crashing into things in the dark, and occasionally peeing in my bedroom closet. My folks became familiar figures at the local hospital's emergency room. If they weren't bringing me in suffering from mysterious high fevers (three of which led to small seizures before I was three), it was because I'd smashed into a wall, headfirst. There are few pictures of me from that time that don't show my face with some self-inflicted bruise or scratch.

I grew into a scrawny child with an unusually big head (my father has described me as "all forehead and gums") and an equally extraordinary amount of energy. No crib or playpen could contain me, and from the time I got my first pair of shoes, I wore them out at a dizzying rate. Without unflinching supervision, I was at constant risk of running out into the street, or worse—and by worse, I'm thinking primarily of the "childproof" bottle of phenobarbital, a barbiturate used to treat seizures, which I pried open and drank at age two.

My world, which at the time meant a small wooden home on a quiet, flat street in a corner of northern Utah, seemed to offer me a limitless supply of targets for mischief, beginning with my siblings, who complain to this day that I rarely managed to walk past any one of them without giving them a poke or a pinch. So of course it wasn't any wonder that by the time I reached the age of five, my mom, who had been parenting the three of us all but round-the-clock, sorely needed a break.

Son of a Square Peg

Now, the last thing I'd want you to assume is that my mother is the type who is *easily* worn down. She's a fast walker and talker who routinely awakes before dawn, and has never once refrained from speaking her mind to my teachers or church authorities alike—a trait I gratefully acknowledge has made a big difference in my own life's trajectory. She's the worthy heir of a line of unusually strong women, although it's also true that a moment of weakness changed her life, when she was just seventeen, and got pregnant with me. She had fallen in love with my dad, Larry Rose, who was studying diesel mechanics on a pole-vaulting scholarship as a freshman at Weber State University. The two of them had talked about marrying someday, but I guess it's fair to say I pushed their plans forward.

Lyda never seriously considered any other option but to drop out of school, putting on hold what had been her vague dreams of following her older sisters into nursing school or finding work as a forest ranger, to become a full-time wife and mother. She waited for a couple of weeks before telling her own mother, my future grandma Ruth Burton, but even then couldn't summon the nerve to do it in person. Instead she left a note on the kitchen table one morning before heading to school. As she recalls, Grandma Burton picked her up at school that afternoon, wearing sunglasses to hide her red eyes. "Lyda, never look back," she told her daughter. "Always look forward." In time, this became my mother's motto, too.

Lyda dropped out of high school while my dad continued in college. He took pride in being the first in his family to graduate from high school and wasn't about to quit now. He began working nights and weekends at a grocery store to support us, meaning that we rarely saw him at home through most of those early years. After getting his diploma, he got a job working with his dad in a truck-repair shop, saving enough money to move us to a two-story home built with a farm loan in a rural town called Hooper. Nor was this the end of his ambition: just a few years later, he reenrolled in school, at night, to pursue a second bachelor's degree, in mechanical engineering.

My dad's father had dropped out in grade school, just after his twelfth birthday, when his folks divorced, and essentially abandoned him. By lying about his age, he got a job in a junkyard, where he slept in an old boxcar at night. Later he worked at a meat-processing plant, and then as a truck driver, while he learned to repair cars on the side. In his own way, he was bright, resilient, and ambitious—traits he passed down to his son.

So in short, I'd describe the Rose family, as of that day I started kindergarten, as flat broke yet determinedly upwardly mobile. Given my parents' shared conviction, still common among American families of that time, that our obstacles would be short-lived, and our lives would eventually be more prosperous than those of previous generations, my mother was therefore cheered to think that not only would she have me off her hands for several hours of the day, during the week, but that my time in the classroom would be well spent. Sure, I was mischievous. Yet based on that preschool test I'd taken, which suggested I was intellectually gifted, the school psychologist assured my mother that there was every reason to expect that I would have a bright future.

Thinking Makes It So

Many years later, as a researcher studying the mechanics of learning, I realized what a powerful advantage I'd had that day at the school door. The tide of my teachers' expectations was poised to carry me to greatness, if only I didn't swim against it.

In recent decades, scientists have offered plenty of evidence to suggest that Hamlet's famous insight—that "there is nothing either good or bad, but thinking makes it so"—can apply to the potentially transformative power of other people's expectations about you. The psychologist Robert Rosenthal, in particular, has produced such convincing evidence of this phenomenon that today it is sometimes referred to as "the Rosenthal effect." He began, as scientists so often do, with rats.

In a study published in 1963, Rosenthal, then a professor at Harvard, assigned several lab rats to a group of his students, telling the students, falsely, that the rats, who were selected at random, had been specially bred for high intelligence. He next assigned another group of rats to another group of students, saying, also falsely, that those animals had been bred for dullness.

The students trained their rats to perform various routine tasks, such as making their way through mazes, and, eventually, just as Rosenthal had expected, the students who had been assigned the supposedly smarter rats reported significantly faster learning times.

Rosenthal next conducted a similar but far more daring experiment, this time involving elementary-school children. With the permission of school administrators in an unnamed, predominantly low-income community in the San Francisco Bay area, he and his colleagues gave students a test, which they later told teachers had revealed that 20 percent of the students were showing "unusual potential for intellectual growth" and could be expected to "bloom" academically by the end of the year. As with the rats, this statement was untrue. Yet, eight years later, when the researchers checked back, the children who had been labeled as ready to bloom had indeed shown a markedly greater increase in performance than those who were not singled out. Rosenthal called this dynamic "the Pygmalion effect," named after the sculptor who, in Greek myth, fell in love with one of his statues. Like Pygmalion, the teachers idealized their charges, and their high hopes became self-fulfilling prophecies.

From my very first week of kindergarten, I was all set to fulfill my teachers' and my parents' hopes, and may well have done just that had it not been for two factors that ultimately proved even more powerful than expectations: my extraordinarily restless disposition and an environment with which I was destined to clash.

A Context of Conformity

Hooper, the small, rural town where I grew up, has long held a place on the far end of the spectrum of traditional Mormon values. Lying just a few miles east of the Great Salt Lake, with a view of the jagged tips of the Wasatch Mountains, it was known as Muskrat Springs for several decades after Brigham Young and his followers first arrived in the state from Illinois, to raise cattle and crops, in the mid-nineteenth century. Today the overwhelming majority of its few thousand residents are proud members of both the Church of Jesus Christ of Latter-day Saints and the Republican Party. (When Ronald Reagan came to Utah in 1982, he drew a crowd of twenty-five thousand to our local park, where he spoke on a podium decorated with a wagon wheel. I was eight years old then and remember running along the edge of the crowd, wearing my free T-shirt that said, "I Had Lunch with Ronnie.") All through my childhood, people put on their best clothes for church on Sunday and stayed dressed up most of the day.

My parents moved to Hooper from the comparatively booming metropolis of nearby Ogden in 1979. My father paid for our small, two-story house with a Farmers Home Administration loan, and my mom grew cucumbers, beans, and corn in the backyard.

Fourteen years later, when my dad could finally afford a bigger house in a livelier neighborhood, my mother made one of her memorable comments. "I want a place with more diversity," she said. "And I don't want to *be* the diversity." What I'm sure she meant was that, from the first, my family had felt like visitors rather than residents in Hooper, a situation that only grew more obvious and awkward over time. Hooper was populated by several families who had lived there as far back as anyone could remember, and to my mother, it seemed as if every kid on the block was someone's cousin, making it extra hard for her children to fit in. My mother, as I've mentioned, was also several degrees more outspoken than most other women in town. Still, what eventually made us pariahs was my own increasingly notorious record as the neighborhood miscreant.

While there was judgment aplenty, however, there were also quite a few upsides to growing up in Hooper for a kid prone to trouble. For starters, it was an extraordinarily safe place—serious crime was all but unheard-of, and most people felt so secure that they routinely left their doors unlocked. Granted, I took some advantage of this particular show of faith, during a phase in which I engaged in some petty breaking-and-entering. But on the whole, I was also protected from several varieties of fear and temptation. I could trust, for instance, that no matter how badly I behaved, my parents would likely stay together. They were both followers of the Mormon faith, which considers marriages binding both on earth and in heaven. And no matter how terribly I treated my siblings, I knew we would stand by each other when it mattered. Perhaps most importantly, throughout my childhood, neither alcohol nor drugs were easily available, nor commonly discussed, reducing risks that might easily have proved too much for me. In fact, when an outsider bought the local store, which was across the street from the elementary school, and had the cluelessness to apply for a liquor license, neighborhood leaders promptly organized a ballot initiative to prevent it.

What made Hooper work so well for most of its residents, in other words, was that very homogeneity that made my white-bread family seem "diverse," in addition to its inhabitants' uncompromising obedience to social norms and religious authority. This combination provided Hooper's residents with structure, predictability, and safety. It also made my failure there inevitable.

Labeled

In my thirteenth year—that infamous year that encompassed both my defeat in the Snickers bar poetry contest and my stink bombs in the art class—our family's pediatrician gave my nonconformity a name: attention deficit/hyperactivity disorder. ADHD is not only one of the most prevalent of childhood mental disorders, but also a leading cause of kids being labeled "troublemakers." Yet despite many decades of well-focused research, it's surprising how often kids who have this label are misunderstood.

The primary characteristics of ADHD include restlessness, forgetfulness, impulsivity, and inattention—traits that most people, and particularly young males, exhibit from time to time, yet which, when severe, can prevent a child from learning, or at least from learning anything in a traditional schoolroom. Scientists have found that many ADHD traits may emerge from a difference with the way a person's brain processes dopamine, an important neurotransmitter or "chemical messenger" that helps alert people to danger and rewards. In other words, dopamine is a motivator, helping us to decide which of the many stimuli that we can attend to at any given time most deserve our attention. Too little of it can lead to difficulty in sustaining attention to matters a person finds uninteresting or irrelevant. And indeed, most people who meet the criteria for ADHD usually have an extremely low tolerance for boredom. Alas, this neurological variability is usually perceived as a character deficit.

It's not as if we restless types enjoy being bored, after all: boredom is in fact a downright painful mental state that is closely related to anxiety. Brain research has demonstrated that, contrary to popular assumption, boredom isn't an inactive mind. In fact, a bored brain is quite busy, seeking stimulation wherever it can find it, sometimes in highly creative and positive ways (to the extent those avenues are available), and also sometimes through risky or provocative behavior such as drug abuse, or, as in my case, provoking my siblings and teachers.

Now, lest you get the impression that I'm entirely against the use of diagnostic "labels," I'm not—so long as they are kept in proper perspective, which includes understanding what they do and do not tell you about your child. At their best, diagnoses can serve useful purposes, such as getting families to think more seriously about their children's highly variable brains, and, ideally, how to make the most of their strengths while minimizing their weaknesses (although when I say "ideally," I mean, that, alas, this all too rarely actually happens). Diagnoses—labels—also help connect people with resources that may often be useful. My caveats are reserved for those all-too-common situations in which parents, teachers, and medical professionals are quick to label someone as "disordered" (whatever that means) when the real problem is a mismatch between a child and a given environment. When the student might in fact function perfectly well in a better school, how fair is it to characterize him or her as defective?

The strategic mistake here boils down to something scientists refer to as a "single-factor fallacy"—the mistaken idea that a problem (such as a delinquent child) can be explained by just one answer. The American physicist Richard Feynman, one of my heroes, once said "I learned very early the difference between knowing the name of something and knowing something." Accordingly, obtaining a diagnosis for a child isn't the same as understanding that child's predicament. Not even close. You may recall from the Prologue that the whole point of complex systems is that they are, indeed, complex, with many variables interacting to produce dramatically different outcomes. This explains both why children diagnosed with behavioral and learning disorders can, just like other kids, have startlingly different futures, and why it's misguided to assume that you simply need to "fix" the child, and everything will be fine.

The answers to understanding and engaging a square-peg student will never be that simple, partly for this important reason: a diagnosis of ADHD won't tell you anything about a child's potential, including how intelligent he or she might be. For example, there's abundant research to show that ADHD symptoms, such as a distractibility and impulsivity, are found in people of all levels of intelligence. In fact, a rather high percentage of so-called gifted children—as many as one in six— also meet the criteria for one or more diagnosable learning challenges.

Snakes and Snails

My grade school environment was a bad match not only for my biological tendencies, but also for my gender, as an increasing amount of research has shown. Of course, school is not an ideal place for girls—not by a long shot—and there are many long-standing gender-specific issues that still need to be addressed for girls to reach their full potential. At the same time, school-age boys, as it turns out, are far more likely to be medicated for attention and learning differences, and to be held back or disciplined for inappropriate behavior. Since the 1980s, boys have trailed girls in reading, writing, grades, test scores, and overall motivation, with increasingly serious effects on their future earning capacity. A recent report went so far as to predict that men will receive less than 40 percent of U.S. college diplomas in 2019, down from 61 percent in 1966.

So, to sum up, there were two major-league strikes against me in school by the time I landed in seventh grade: I was diagnosed with ADHD, and I was a boy. Making matters even worse by that seventh-grade year was that I was an adolescent boy. Adolescent boys have filled the ranks of troublemakers throughout history. As Leo Tolstoy wrote, "I have read somewhere that children from 12 to 14 years of age . . . are singularly inclined to arson and even murder. As I look back upon my boyhood, I can quite appreciate the possibility of the most frightful crime being committed without object or intent to injure but just because—out of curiosity, or to satisfy an unconscious craving for action."

Becoming Cain

Call me precocious, but Tolstoy's description of the adolescent male would have applied to me roughly by the age of three. I'm thinking in particular about the time when I pushed my little sister, Kim, out of our second-story window, purportedly to see if she could fly.

The backstory was that I was already sick and tired of hearing how my calm, compliant little sister, who always slept through the night and never got into trouble, was Mommy's precious "angel"—sent from heaven, as I remember her crooning, to make her life easier. I'd learned about "real" angels at church, which I guess helps explain the irresistible impulse that took hold of me one afternoon when my mother was busy cooking dinner and I spotted Kim leaning on the window screen.

A minute later, I ran to the kitchen, shouting to my mother: "Guess what? Kim doesn't have wings!"

This would be one of the first of what turned out to be a frankly hair-raising number of narrow escapes by the time I reached young adulthood. By only just a few inches, Kim missed hitting the concrete pavement below. Instead she landed in the shrubbery, scratched but intact. What might have been a horrifying event that would have changed all of our lives forever miraculously played out instead as a funny story that we still tell each other at family reunions.

Another of our family's best-loved tales also involves me and Kim. We were both still in preschool, and, in a highly unusual instance, were left unsupervised one afternoon long enough for me to fetch the spray paint I'd seen in our garage and spray stick-figure drawings all over our house's concrete foundation in the backyard. I'd assumed it would all wash away with the garden hose, but when it didn't, I thought fast, remembering how Kim always drew little circles for kneecaps on her figures. I filled them in on mine just in time before my mother appeared and

Kim took the fall. Several years would pass before I confessed to the crime to my parents, who had of course figured it all out anyway by then.

These antics were rapidly earning me a reputation in my extended family and our tight-knit neighborhood in Hooper, where everyone was closely involved in everyone else's business. My many aunts and uncles were soon referring to me as "Cain." Long before I started grade school, in other words, I was acquiring a reputation that would dog me for nearly two decades, as I left in my wake a broad swath of misunderstandings, hurt feelings, school failures, and bodily harm.

As I've gradually come to realize, however, it could have been much worse. Worn-out, exasperated, and inexperienced as my mother was, as a twenty-three-year-old high-school dropout consumed by caring for several small children, she also brought her own unique disposition to the mix: a blend of independence, imagination, and passion that ultimately led to her boldly out-of-the-box way of parenting me. Almost as if she were drawing from the study of complex systems, she in time came to appreciate that even as I was so often branded a troublemaker, and even as I was most certainly contributing to that reputation, the causes of the trouble I got into routinely extended beyond my control. Through the years, she had to learn and grow and be much more discerning than the average parent about just how much power she could wield over my behavior, and when she needed to look elsewhere in my environment. Nor, at least after the first few years, did she take my bad behavior as a personal indictment, which in particular, distinguished her as well ahead of her time.

Nature, Nurture, and Blaming the Moms

This takes some explaining. In the 1970s, when my mother was starting her family, moms of kids with any number of differences and challenges were under terrible fire. Psychologists preached, and most people believed, that parents—meaning moms—were the major cause of homosexuality, autism, schizophrenia, and the kinds of behavioral problems that might, for example, predispose a toddler to push his little sister out a window.

"If your child was gay, that meant you were overbearing; if he was always misbehaving, it meant that you weren't disciplining him enough," my mother has since recalled. "And it was all, all, aimed at the moms. Nothing stuck to the dads: they were Teflon-coated."

The judgment was often as heartless as it was unscientific: in the 1950s, the famous psychologist and author Bruno Bettelheim championed the notion that cold and withdrawn "refrigerator mothers" were responsible for their children's autism. Bettelheim went so far as to compare these mostly exhausted and overwhelmed parents to Nazi concentration camp guards.

No wonder, nearly two decades later, that so many mothers were vastly relieved when the pendulum swung sharply in the other direction. After years of breakthrough findings about genetic influences on behavior, a new creed of biological determinism all but absolved parents of responsibility for shaping their children's future and held out the hope that scientists would one day find a single gene for each learning difference, from dyslexia to ADHD.

The truth, of course, falls somewhere in between these two extremes.

The work of behavioral geneticist Robert Plomin, regarded as one of the hundred most eminent psychologists of our era, in my view best conveys that complicated middle road, based on his studies of data involving some fifteen thousand sets of twins. Plomin has shown that when it comes to learning and behavioral differences (including what we now call "disorders"), there's no one gene that causes any of them. Rather, a vast assortment of genes that may predispose a child toward such a difference get turned on or off as they interact with a unique (Plomin coined the term "nonshared") family and social environment. Each sibling, he posits, grows up in an essentially different family, which explains why each grows up to be such a different adult. Rather than talk about "nature or nurture," Plomin insists on the phrase "nature *and* nurture."

This modern model—that learning and behavioral differences result from an interaction between genetic predispositions and environments—offers parents of children like I was a real hope that we will be able to redirect our kids from paths that create disability and disorder. Because so many genes are involved, each with only a tiny individual impact, it is clear that genetic engineering can't be the solution. So, while neuroscience and genetics will continue to inform our understanding of differences, most of the work we need to do must be in influencing environments, such as the ways that parents raise their kids, and teachers teach them.

There are many examples of the power of this perspective,

but for now I'll give you just one. In 2004, Terrie Moffitt, a professor at King's College in London and a colleague of Robert Plomin, reported on a study of more than 2,200 five-year-old twins, half of whom had low birth weight, a common precursor to a diagnosis of ADHD. Moffitt and her colleagues found that the low-birth-weight babies who had more warm and loving relationships with their mothers were less likely to be described as having ADHD symptoms by parents and teachers years later. In other words, a warm, accepting, positive environment helped "buffer" these vulnerable children from the kinds of ADHD-like characteristics to which they were predisposed by genetic and intrauterine influences.

Moffitt's report, published in the *Journal of Counseling and Clinical Psychology,* provoked a surprisingly angry reaction from more biology-centered researchers, including a scathing public letter by the ADHD expert psychiatrist Russell Barkley, who questioned Moffitt's methods and complained that her study "blames the mother."

Moffitt and her colleagues defended the research at the time yet eventually decided the risks of more controversy outweighed the benefits of pursuing it. I find that a pity. Setting aside my discomfort, as a scientist, at seeing research effectively censored, I believe parents urgently need more of just this kind of help in alerting them to ways they can modify their children's environments when called for by biological predispositions.

Restorative Niches

I was blessed that my mother avoided tilting to either extreme during the nature-nurture pendulum swings of her time. She neither punished me unmercifully, yet nor did she ever surrender her power. Instead she hung in with me through a series of embarrassments and frustrations, trying to guide me as best she could, while not taking my screw-ups personally.

In recent years, I've often asked my mom how she came by her self-confidence. Her answer always includes a reference to her faith. "I read the Bible in the afternoons while my kids took naps," she says. "This helped me feel peace, which I needed once they woke up!" She says her faith gave her a perspective that allowed her to trust her own instincts and that the combination of the two fortified her in the face of all the criticism that came her way.

Beyond faith, my mom also relied on traditional comforts to help pull her through. For example, when my siblings and I were small, my mother unfailingly showed up for a thrice-weekly, 5:30 a.m. aerobics class, while the rest of the family slept. There she not only got exercise but also routinely socialized with a group of her like-minded friends—a practice social scientists recommend as a boost for well-being. She also talked on the phone several times a week to her least judgmental sister, whom I'll call Jane. Such habits constitute what my colleague Brian Little, who studies human flourishing, has described as "restorative niches," and I'm sure they helped keep my mother sane through the many trials I obliged her to endure over the next decade and more.

BIG IDEAS
• • • • • • • • • •

- Learning differences, temperament, and other human characteristics are the product of neither nature nor nurture alone, but of a complex dynamic of the two.
- As the Rosenthal effect demonstrates, performance can be dramatically influenced by the expectations of others (including parents and teachers). Keep this in mind and never let a label diminish what you think your child is capable of accomplishing.
- ADHD, like other learning and behavioral "disorders," remains a vexingly vague diagnosis, and it is most helpful when viewed as a starting point (not a solution) for understanding your child's unique strengths and weaknesses, and finding appropriate support.
- Mothers do not "cause" schizophrenia, homosexuality, autism, or ADHD. But neither are these or any other human conditions purely caused by genes. A child's environment, including his or her parenting, will always strongly influence his or her future.

ACTION ITEMS
• ▪ • ▪ • ▪ • ▪ • ▪ • ▪ •

▪ Keep hugging your kid.

▪ Don't ever leave curious, hyperactive, impulsive toddlers unsupervised near younger sisters, open windows, and/or bottles of barbiturates.

▪ Forget what you've heard about biological determinism. Of course, biology matters, but parents and teachers can influence a child's development in many subtle, positive, and important ways.

▪ Make sure to find your own "restorative niches"—if possible including regular doses of exercise and friendship. They're useful for everyone, but downright essential for parents of struggling square-peg kids.

Smart Criminal

"We are all special cases."

—ALBERT CAMUS

Out of Control

"What were you thinking?" I heard my dad yell from the other side of our front lawn, on what until just a minute earlier had been a peaceful, muggy summer night.

I can still hear the anger and surprise in his voice, and still feel the hot shame creeping up my neck. I was nine years old, and this felt like the moment my identity was sealed: I was, and always would be, a hopeless square peg.

My mom and dad had been barbecuing dinner for a dozen or so aunts and uncles and cousins. We kids were hanging around on the sidewalk, swatting mosquitoes, when for some reason, which may have boiled down to simple boredom, I picked up a rock and threw it at a passing car.

Just as when I threw those stink bombs four years later, there was no good reason for what I did, and plenty of good reasons not to have done it. I'd never before met the driver of the rust-colored car—a dark-haired man about my dad's age. Nor was I angry about anything in particular at the time, at least that I can recall. Throwing that rock just seemed like the thing I had to do.

Maybe I thought it would be funny. Back then, I thought a lot of things were funny that most other people found simply annoying. According to some researchers, I suppose I was desperately seeking stimulation—that, and I was also the kind of kid who, even after I realized something wasn't that great an idea after all, had a lot of trouble putting on the brakes.

In some contexts, this generally hastier MO can be an advantage. Athletes, for instance, hone their reaction times on purpose. Artists can also benefit. Consider an improv actor on a stage, on the spot to come up with material. He'll never hit the high notes if his mental brakes are too efficient, making him censor his wildest ideas.

In the context of Hooper, however, my impulsivity offered no boon. More and more, in fact, and even within my extended family, I was being shunned because of it. I wasn't athletic or creative back then: I was simply annoying.

I used to make a practice, for example, of eating every single Popsicle my mom brought home before anyone else could get to them. I also used to twist my brothers' nipples when they tried to slip past me in the hallways. Sometimes when I caught them, I'd pin them on their backs as I let a stream of spit slowly dribble from my lips, so that if they moved the least bit, they'd get slimed.

My four siblings and I are the best of friends today, yet there are few family reunions that don't include an hour or so of them sitting around telling stories about all the awful things I used to do to them. Among my most notorious deeds is the time I dragged my brother Doug out of the shower one winter night and locked him, naked, in the snow outside our front door. I remember that well, except for the part about why I did it. There was also a summer day at the neighborhood park when it struck me how hilarious it would be to pull down my pants and pee down the slide. So that's what I did, after which neither I nor any of the Rose kids was ever allowed back.

My point here is that long before I reached my teens, I'd morphed from a bright but hyperactive child into an increasingly unpopular pest. What was once seen as my harmless childhood quirkiness had come to be viewed as permanently bad character.

Who needed more proof that I was a bad seed than my throwing the rock at that stranger's car?

Tsk-tsking away, my aunts and uncles gathered around the scene of the crime like gnats, as the driver, who'd swerved to the curb, jumped out to inspect the small new dent on the passenger side of his car.

Before I could answer my father—and what would I have said, given that the point is that I *wasn't* thinking?—I heard my mom's sister, Betty, pipe up, with her way of addressing everyone and no one in particular: "At least my kids can control themselves."

Aunt Betty has several children of her own, and she was right about one thing: as far back as I can remember, they have always been much better behaved than I. Still, it wasn't until that moment that I fully grasped the point that she had already made on several previous occasions, which was that I really couldn't control myself. I didn't want to be in trouble all the time, but somehow I kept doing things that got me there.

Making matters worse was my increasing tendency to dig in my heels whenever I got caught. I did that again on the night of the barbecue. Rather than apologize for throwing that rock, I turned to my dad, and for some crazy reason coolly replied, "Actually, I was trying to hit his window—but I missed."

Hearing this, Aunt Betty raised her eyebrows at my mother, while the car owner walked up huffily to my father.

"Sir, your child is a delinquent," he sputtered, after which he turned around, got back in his car, and sped off.

Now, anyone listening to all of this might have fairly assumed that I was not only a bad kid, and maybe not that bright, after all, but also intent on self-destruction. What in the world would make a boy invite the world's bad opinion like that?

A Rebel by Choice

It has taken me many years to understand my bad attitude then, but here's what I eventually realized: I was terrified—less by any threat of punishment than by the frightening possibility of some truth in Aunt Betty's take on me: that I really couldn't control my own hands. If that were true, I'd be a spastic, a retard, and all the other terrible things kids were already calling me at school.

Okay, it's not like I hadn't given them some cause. I may never, for instance, live down the time, in a tenth-grade basketball game, that I scored the winning point—for the other team. That infamous occasion was only the most dramatic example of the kinds of weird screw-ups in which I was constantly involved. Every day, and sometimes many times a day, I'd do something I'd later regret. In the classroom, for instance, I could always be counted on to blurt out often-irrelevant comments and wise-cracks alike, a habit both my teacher and classmates found obnoxious.

Only much later did I understand that I did this not only because I'm impulsive, but also because I have exceedingly poor short-term, or "working" memory.

As it turns out, working memory—the ability to hold information temporarily in your mind while you're doing something else—is hugely important in all dimensions of your life. Research has shown that it is one of the most important predictors of academic achievement, which starts to make sense when you consider how you need to retain information even for the simplest mathematical problems (that's 21; so put down the 1, carry the 2 . . .). Bad news for me, since as tests would later show, I rank somewhere near the bottom second percentile for all Americans in working memory.

My limited working memory capacity got me on the wrong track from my earliest years in school, and kept me there; yet today I'm convinced that it needn't really be such a huge academic liability. By not understanding how much people vary in their working memory, teachers today force kids constantly to jump through needless hoops, much as if they were obliging their students to ride unicycles between classes. Were that the case, a kid who was a budding genius at math but hopelessly uncoordinated might never be able to get to his class and show what he could do.

While, of course, few teachers would seriously consider such a system, many require the cognitive equivalent, with unnecessary rules that often create learning problems where none had existed. It's more the pity, since schools could easily make many simple changes to get rid of those cognitive unicycles and stop squandering kids' precious memory capacity.

One such easy step would be to routinely make sure that both class schedules and the goal of any exercise being worked on at the time are always available to students on the blackboard, thereby reducing the information they need to hold in their minds. Another (albeit more expensive) step would be to provide two sets of textbooks, so kids can keep one set at home and not have to remember to bring them back and forth. Teachers can also learn to avoid issuing unnecessary multiple-step instructions ("Take out your books; turn to page forty-three, and underline the paragraph that starts with . . .").

Poor working memory does more than threaten academic success; it's also terrible for social relationships. I was so unskillful at the basic art of following conversations—trying to listen to what was being said, while keeping in mind what I wanted to say—that I'd often strike others as if I didn't care what they had on their minds. I'd blurt things out, interrupting schoolmates and teachers during class, out of uncontrollable anxiety that if I didn't, I'd forget it.

My working memory difficulties made me unreliable, spoiling people's trust in me again and again. I'd make a new friend, but then forget some crucial detail about that person and seem like I didn't care. I'd spend hours doing homework, but then forget to bring it to school. I constantly lost homework assignments, field trip forms, sweaters, gym clothes, and lunch boxes. In return, my parents, who had so little extra cash to replace all these items, lost their patience.

Whenever I wasn't caught red-handed at some impulsive prank or act of unintentional forgetfulness, I'd do my best to cover my tracks, no matter how much I had to lie. But at some point, quite possibly on the night I threw that rock, I made a decision. I'd "own" my screw-ups and crimes, for the simple reason that other people's annoyance and even contempt was much better than their pity and rejection. Playing the outlaw at least made me feel I had some control.

Anything but Helpless

Only much later, after I went to school and studied psychology, did I come to appreciate the perverse wisdom of my choice, given what seemed like my limited options. By the age of nine, I'd had enough experience out in the world to feel like a chronic failure, and so little experience of being in control of my behavior that I was dangerously close to falling into a mental trap psychologists call "learned helplessness." This condition is a poignant example of the kind of negative feedback loop I told you about at the start of this book, and about which I will have a lot more to say in future chapters, in which a negative outcome leads to a negative response, and so on, in an excruciatingly vicious cycle that can lead to a cascade of problems.

The now-formidable body of research on learned helplessness began in the 1960s when the psychologist Martin Seligman, then at the University of Pennsylvania, conducted a series of experiments with dogs. In one of the trials, he and his colleagues compared the reactions of two groups of dogs that were given painful electric shocks. One group was able to end the shocks by pressing a lever, but the other dogs' levers didn't have any effect. As it turned out, the dogs that were able to control their experience escaped any lasting psychological harm, but the dogs that were helpless in the face of those arbitrary punishments turned passive. They lay down on the floor of the electrified cage and took the shocks, even when moving two feet would end them.

Seligman would later propose that depressed people might be helped by being carefully guided through experiences in which they learned to exert increasing control over their environments, reversing their past experience. And as other researchers confirmed his findings in different studies, he expanded his message to advise parents that providing children with early experiences teaching them that they have the power to influence their world can help inoculate them against depression in later life.

My own early experiences, combined with what I've learned from this line of research, have convinced me that many a child's choice of "bad" behavior over surrendering to powerlessness might well be a healthy survival tactic—and that if we as adults can understand it as such, we can judge less and help a lot more. Now, I don't mean that we should ignore bad behavior—of course we shouldn't—but short-term punishment of the behavior will never be more effective than tactics based on an understanding of the reason for that behavior. As it is, sadly, misguided efforts by kids to fight against their rising sense of helplessness are most often misunderstood and simply punished.

For several weeks after my starring role at the barbecue, Aunt Betty lobbied my mother to take me to a psychiatrist. "I don't mean to tell you what to do," she lectured. "But I would seriously think about it. It may not be Todd's fault that he is that way."

While this wasn't actually a bad idea, my mom struggled to put it out of her mind as long as she could. For one thing, it was clear that her sister's comment wasn't meant to be helpful, but more like her way of pouring salt on a wound. That aside, at the time my mother didn't see how she could possibly afford therapy. Once I started middle school a few years later, however, and my mom could see how I was failing to cope with the increasing homework load and social pressures, she started to save up money and ask around for referrals. At very least, she would see if I qualified for a diagnosis.

From my point of view, my behavior was easy to understand: I was simply reacting reasonably to what I perceived as other people being mean to me. And of course, the worse I behaved, the meaner they all were.

My brothers and sisters, for instance, had long ago learned how to provoke me with sinister efficiency. They called me "Toad" and "ree-tard," whispering behind my mother's back, at which point I'd lunge at them, and they'd cry, and I'd end up being the only one punished. They felt that was only fair, not only because of how much I'd bullied them personally, but because of how everything I did reflected on them, getting them banned from neighborhood pools, parks, and parties.

Home, in other words, wasn't exactly a haven for me, although school was much worse. By sixth grade I'd lost all my former friends, and day after day I faced the humiliation of having no one to sit next to at lunch. Kids teased me and teachers nagged me, complaining that I was disruptive and wouldn't follow instructions. When I recall today how most people reacted to me back then, I recognize that while there were times when it was clear that I was in the wrong, just as there were times where I was clearly unjustly treated, these extremes were exceptions. Instead, much of the time I probably missed cues and misunderstood directions, in subtle ways that made people think I was rude, willful, and lazy. Given that I had no clue why I affected other people like that, I got used to feeling like a victim, even when others characterized me as a villain.

A Bad Fit

You may have already figured out by now that for a kid like I used to be, sitting still and minding my own business for hour after hour in a classroom would be a special challenge. And you would have figured right. Even as an adult, I find it excruciatingly painful to endure even the few minutes of obligatory lull in a movie theater before the previews begin. Yet this is nothing compared to the soul-crushing tedium prevalent in most U.S. classrooms.

We adults tend to forget the enormous amount of time that dragged by when we were students, as teachers passed out papers or spoke individually with our classmates. But from time to time we get stirring reminders. After systematically following fifty-two high school boys, who were either high achieving, run-of-the-mill, or struggling academically through their daily routines in U.S. public school classrooms, the author and education reformer Jeffrey Wilhelm concluded that boredom, which he called "an underestimated force in education," was responsible for "everything from bullying to dropping out."

Throughout the United States, with very few exceptions, most schools still follow the old-fashioned model: a teacher stands in front of students sitting in neat lines of desks, with their textbooks opened before them. This helps explain why the writer and former psychotherapist Thom Hartmann calls ADHD, with its extreme intolerance for boredom, a "context disorder." That's probably closer to the truth, in my opinion.

Not surprisingly, few if any classrooms in rural Utah questioned this model of conformity in the years I was growing up. The mere fact that I was left-handed struck a few of my most doctrinaire grade school teachers as, literally, satanic. I never felt much difference, in fact, between sitting in school and sitting in church. In both settings, the authority vested in the adult in charge was absolute. In both settings, kids were expected to sit silently while contemplating what Harvard's Kurt Fischer refers to as the "holy book." In both settings, despite all the effort I'd make to control myself, I'd ultimately, continually, disturb the peace.

The cognitive scientist David Rose (who is a colleague, but not a family member) says that for all the reasons I've mentioned, boring schools are the perfect bad match for kids with short attention spans and a low tolerance for boredom. "We not only don't educate them—we damage them," he says.

At the very least, we give many millions of kids the message they have to change their biology—their very nature—to fit into the rigid environment of school. The pediatrician who first diagnosed me with ADHD gave my mom a prescription for the stimulant Ritalin, the most common treatment, then and now, for restless square pegs. I took the pills on and off for the next three years, with some early success. Taking the drug initially helped me get A's and kind words from teachers during my first semester in seventh grade. Yet whenever I stopped, my grades plummeted, and my teachers returned to complaining.

While I recognized the benefits, that didn't stop me from hating the Ritalin. It made my sleep problems even worse and reduced my appetite a bit, but most important to me, it made me feel I couldn't be "normal" without medication. More often than not, I just faked taking the pills and threw them away—especially after the humiliating tenth-grade drama class in which my teacher once shouted: "For the love of God, Todd, didn't you take your pill today?" Indeed, I hadn't.

When I turned sixteen, my mother had the foresight and initiative to do something that was avant-garde for that time, the year 1990. She drove me to Salt Lake City for a neuropsychological evaluation by a psychologist, Sam Goldstein, who, after a few hours of testing and interviews, confirmed the initial diagnosis of ADHD and, crucially, helped her along on her path of understanding more about my puzzling behavior. (As part of his inquiry, for instance, Goldstein sent questionnaires to three of my teachers, who observed me both on and off stimulants. They all thought I was fine on the Ritalin, yet when I wasn't medicated, all three rated me above the 98th percentile in "hyperkinetic behavior," noting "severe" problems with "restlessness, unpredictable behavior, distractibility, inattention, disturbing others, excitability, impulsivity, failing to finish things and being easily frustrated in his efforts.")

In contrast to my busy pediatrician, who diagnosed me in the standard manner—taking about a half hour to analyze written responses from my mother and me to an itemized checklist of symptoms—Goldstein provided my mother with a ten-page report that detailed some of my strengths and weaknesses. Among other things—and this is common for many kids like me—he discovered a 14-point gap between my verbal IQ and my academic performance. Something was getting in the way—something that Goldstein suggested was at least in part a mix of my attention deficit and my resultant anxiety.

As awareness of learning and behavioral differences increases, this type of extensive neuropsychological evaluation is becoming increasingly popular as an initial step for parents of children with suspected learning challenges. The chief obstacle for most parents is the expense, combined with the fact that so few insurance plans cover such exams. Schools are supposed to provide thorough testing, as long as there's good reason to believe a child is struggling with a learning impairment. My mother never tried to get my school to pay, assuming she'd be turned down. But she later told me that she felt the information she received was worth the expense, since it armed her to face anyone—teachers, family members, and even know-it-all neighbors—for years to come, whenever they suggested that my bad behavior was due to bad character.

Lyda on Her Own

My mother, as I've understood only in recent years, needed all the support she could get. While of course I wasn't the only young troublemaking square peg in Hooper, mothers of such kids as a rule didn't confide in each other. That would be airing dirty laundry, advertising the failures they couldn't help but feel were their fault.

In those years, in other parts of the country, parents of kids whose learning differences clashed with their school system were starting to form support groups. For example, CHADD (Children and Adults with Attention Deficit/Hyperactivity Disorder) launched its first chapter in Plantation, Florida, in 1987, eventually gathering thousands of members throughout the nation over the next decade. It would have been nice for Lyda if something like that existed in Hooper, during her hard slog through the 1980s. As she has since told me, she would have been on-her-knees grateful for even one friend or neighbor to say, "I don't understand what you're going through, but how can I help?" Or at school, if someone said, "Let's work on this together. What can we do to help him?" Lyda says, "Everyone had an opinion about what I should be doing, but I'd have jumped for joy if they'd just said something like that."

On top of the lack of empathy was a lack of useful data. Most pediatricians knew next to nothing about the characteristics of ADHD or other learning issues, let alone what could be done to support these kids. Netscape, the first Internet browser, was launched only in 1995, and it would be several years after that before decent websites about these issues existed.

This makes me all the more impressed by my mom's resolve to educate herself. In fact, I'm pretty sure she got a kick out of all that learning she was doing—not just about me, but about her family and herself. From her conversations with Goldstein, she understood for the first time that the characteristics of ADHD, like so many other basic ways of reacting to the world, usually begin with a genetic legacy that predisposes a child to certain behaviors, which are then shaped by that child's environment. She suddenly saw the legacy throughout her family tree, most dramatically in the case of her big brother, Bob, a troublemaker who not only failed all his classes but drank, smoked, and roamed the streets late at night, and eventually landed in reform school for burglarizing a church. Several years later, Bob found happiness as a long-haul trucker, which Lyda took as a hopeful sign that even the squarest of pegs can find contexts that suit them.

Moreover, after seeing Bob in this new light, Lyda reconsidered her own restless life, a process that led her to the realization that she and I weren't so different. Like me, she gets bored easily and loves to go on adventures, such as traveling to exotic places. She can't sit for any length of time without jiggling her foot, and, while, unlike me, she has always been a dedicated Mormon, she has never been the unquestioning kind. When I was still in high school in Hooper, for example, my mom gained a certain local notoriety for being the only member of the town council to publicly oppose a new pig farm that was stinking up our neighborhood. Unlike her colleagues on that august body, she didn't think it was relevant that the farm was owned by a prominent member of the local lay Mormon leadership. What mattered to her was that the smelly business violated the zoning laws, so she pursued the issue until it was shut down. Her picture appeared in the local newspaper; she made enemies among the farmer's many allies, and through it all appeared to thoroughly enjoy herself. Similarly, I suspect she got at least a little thrill, at least on some occasions, from going to battle on my behalf with adults she thought misunderstood me.

Education for All?

While Lyda was educating herself about the nature and nurture of learning differences, so—albeit much more slowly—was the rest of America. A lot of this awakening was forced on the country as a series of lawsuits and federal legislation led to fundamental change in what at least some parents could expect from schools. The changes began by addressing the gravest injustices: for most of the twentieth century, children with major disabilities—such as being blind, deaf, or labeled "emotionally disturbed" or "mentally retarded"—were explicitly excluded from public schools. As a result, an estimated one million U.S. children, many of whom might have benefited from mainstream schools with minor amounts of support, had no access to free education, while another 3.5 million were segregated in substandard programs.

Beginning in the 1970s, however, federal legislation cleared the way for the "mainstreaming" of students with physical and mental handicaps, a policy officially adopted in 1990 when Congress passed the Individuals with Disabilities Education Act (IDEA). Amendments to the act seven years later guaranteed all children the right to a "free, appropriate" education in the "least restrictive environment" possible.

Today, more than six million U.S. children are receiving some sort of special educational support under this law and through parallel legislation stemming from Section 504 of the 1973 Rehabilitation Act. The kinds of support offered ranges from training teachers in special education to providing aides for students who need them, to sometimes even paying private tuition for kids who can't get a "free, appropriate" education in public schools, to such relatively minor accommodations as giving kids with learning challenges more time to work on tests.

On the one hand, I'm moved by how much we've learned, as a nation, in barely three decades, and how much more support children can receive in schools today. On the other hand, I'm surprised at the depth of ignorance that remains. For example, one national poll, published in October 2010, reported that a majority of Americans still believe that learning disabilities are a "product of the home environment." We've still got a long way to go.

Considering the continuing prevalence of public ignorance about learning differences, I cringe to imagine what it was like for my mom in rural Utah, twenty years ago. She tells me that, for the most part, it was much easier to cope with outright criticism from the people she knew didn't care about me than it was to fend off advice from people determined to be helpful—in other words, the well-wishers. My dad's mom, for instance, who was staunchly opposed to "unnatural" pharmaceutical stimulants, insisted on providing me with herbal milk shakes produced by the Utah-based Sunrider Corporation. My mom yielded to pressure, and I drank the awful shakes for a few months, until it was clear to all concerned that they weren't changing my behavior. A few years later, we learned that the Utah Department of Agriculture had closed the company's plant, after finding that the soybeans they imported from China were tainted with salmonella.

Fending off her mother-in-law was hard enough for Lyda. Resisting my father's parenting strategy, as much as she disagreed with it, was unfortunately often beyond her.

Hurt

When I think back on it, it's easy for me today to see just how much my dad always loved me, even during the darkest of my childhood years. Alas, however, it wasn't always so.

Granted, all through my increasingly challenging adolescence, he was doing his best to provide for our family, against daunting odds, and under mounting stress. Having graduated college by taking classes at night, my dad was at this point working as a mechanic at the shop his father managed, while earning about ten dollars an hour. His many hours of overtime were the only reason we managed to hold onto the house.

Worried, harassed, and reeking of oil and hydraulic fuel, my dad would come home late in the evenings, only to hear the latest discouraging news from my mother about how I'd failed another class, or stolen money from her purse, or tormented my siblings, or left a bag of flaming poo on a neighbor's doorstep, inciting the unlucky recipient to stomp out the flames (note: this really works like it does in the movies . . . amazing!). All the while, his image of my future grew sharper and darker. "I knew Todd was smart, I just thought he would be a smart criminal!" he told one interviewer, in what has to be one of my all-time favorite quotes—and one that I've teased him about throughout the years.

My father never followed my mother on her trips to the doctors with me, partly because he was either at work or in school, but also because he never bought the paradigm of me as a patient who needed curing. His own diagnosis of my behavior was simple: I was a budding juvenile delinquent, who needed a stronger hand—literally. Throughout my teens, this fear drove an otherwise gentle man to mimic his own dad's parenting, which featured more yelling and spanking than encouragement or advice. Physical punishment never seemed like a good strategy to Lyda, however, and she wasn't afraid to tell my father so. This caused a lot of arguments between them, with my dad accusing her of coddling me and failing to "set limits."

While my mother didn't win every parenting argument, nor did she back down. Instead she took a parenting course, read everything she could about learning differences, and argued ever more adamantly that I needed more encouragement, and less criticism and punishment. "Todd was dying inside, and for a while, I didn't get that," she'd recall, many years later. "But I finally decided that this kid cannot be attacked everywhere. I had to change at least what happened between him and me."

Only as an adult did I fully appreciate my mom's efforts in this respect. Strong-willed as she was, and is, it still couldn't have been easy to oppose my dad's approach to teaching me discipline, particularly given how popular physical punishment was (and still is) across the United States. Studies show that most American families believe that spanking is good for kids, despite the fact that research has clearly established that, as normally practiced, it's ineffective at best and counterproductive at worst—particularly for kids like I was then.

It's perversely easy for a parent to be seduced into physical punishment. It can feel, at least in the moment, like you're taking control, teaching a lesson, and showing your child who's boss. And in fact, at least some research does suggest that under precisely controlled conditions (in terms of timing, intensity, and duration), physical punishment may be effective. Realistically, however, few if any parents can manage to get all these variables right in a heated situation. So instead, what kids usually get is slaps, spankings, and beatings delivered in anger, and resulting in no positive change in their behavior. My mom later told me she could see that spankings never made me better, but were rather merely an outlet for my dad's fear and frustration.

Just as important, when parents resort to beatings over long periods of time, it diminishes their influence, leading to what psychologists call "avoidance behavior." Humans, in other words, just like all other animals, naturally seek to avoid pain, and by extension, other people and situations that cause it. Thus, unfortunately, my dad's parenting strategies pushed me away just when I needed him the most.

Beatings do more than damage relationships. Repeated corporal punishment can do lasting harm to a child's developing brain, flooding the system with stress hormones that cause changes to critical brain structures involved in such important processes as social cognition, self-perception, and working memory. Sustained beatings can also make kids more aggressive and impair their capacity for self-control—a particularly poignant negative feedback loop, given that so many kids are initially punished for just those failures.

All this comes on top of the fact that physical punishment simply isn't effective when the intent is to curb impulsive and absentminded behaviors that the child can't control, such as my throwing the rock at the car, or forgetting to bring home my homework assignment. I'm not suggesting kids be allowed to get away with bad behavior—simply that the research clearly demonstrates that physical punishment is so often self-defeating. Honestly, at that point in my life, you could have chained me to a wall and whipped me and it wouldn't have prevented most of the dumb things I was doing.

Pulling Me Closer

As modern researchers might have predicted, therefore, by the time I started middle school I feared my father, avoided him as best I could, and had become all but incapable of listening to anything he had to say. To the best of my ability, I sided with my mother, the "good cop." I don't want to give the impression that Lyda never lost her temper—I'm fairly sure that kids like I was back then could bring out the child abuser in Mother Teresa. There were times, as I recall, when my mother would chase me through the house with a flyswatter. But these were exceptions, not the rule.

As I entered my teens, Lyda could see I'd fallen into a hole. My self-confidence was failing, after years of friends abandoning me for reasons I couldn't figure out, and teachers telling me to try harder when I was already trying as hard as I thought I could.

Once she realized this, my mother decided that she was going to show me as much love and appreciation and support as she possibly could, counterintuitive as it might have seemed.

Now, let me be clear—Lyda was not a pushover, not even close, and she had no intention of coddling me. She was smarter than that, and I'm convinced that, all else being equal, she would have been every bit as demanding of me as my father. She expected respect, discipline, and responsibility from her kids, just as he did, but she recognized in my case, and at that time, there were other ways to accomplish the goal.

She managed to see through my bluster to understand that what I needed the most—at that moment in my life—was a relationship in which I could feel genuinely safe and valued. So no matter how badly I behaved, she was determined to keep me close. Again, it did not mean "anything goes," and I was punished when she felt I deserved it. But at the same time, she worked hard to control her anger, as best she could, and to find things in me to praise, from the questions I asked to my abilities on the basketball court.

Everything I've learned since then has confirmed Lyda's wisdom. Today, I tell parents that the number-one thing to keep in mind, challenging as it may be sometimes, is to preserve a good relationship with your child. Set limits, sure. Teach responsibility—of course! But remember that parenting is more like chess than checkers. There are always multiple ways to achieve your goals, and you have to be adaptive, always thinking three steps ahead. Sometimes being as strict as a cop is the right thing to do, yet there will be times where giving your child unconditional love is the better strategy—rules be damned.

BIG IDEAS
• ▪ • ▪ • ▪ • ▪ •

- Beware of well-wishers: Just because they care doesn't mean they always know best—especially when it comes to nutritional milk shakes.

- Sometimes the most resilient of square-peg kids will choose to be seen as rebels, rather than out of control or helpless.

- Conventional school environments are a particularly bad match for kids with short attention spans and low thresholds for boredom.

- The quality of a child's working memory is a powerful predictor of his or her academic success.

- The research is clear on physical punishment. Beatings and spankings don't work well in changing children's behavior, and can also risk lasting harm to a child's relationship with his parents and his developing brain.

ACTION ITEMS
• ▪ • ▪ • ▪ • ▪ • ▪ • ▪ •

▪ Stop hugging your kid, already. It's starting to creep him out! Take a chapter off.

▪ Repeat the mantra: smart parenting is like chess, not checkers.

▪ Evaluate the demands in your child's life (at home and at school)—and find at least one "cognitive unicycle" that may be sabotaging him or her. Then, if you can, get rid of it.

▪ Investigate potential support organizations in your area (or nationally), and consider joining one if it seems appropriate for your goals and needs. My personal favorite is a San Francisco–based grassroots group called Parents Education Network (PEN). For other parts of the country, try Googling the words "support," your hometown, and your child's diagnosis, if there is one.

▪ You can help a child with poor working memory learn coping strategies for school, and also guide his or her teacher to adopt some easy guidelines to prevent that deficit from becoming a handicap. For instance, encourage your child to write down his or her thoughts, rather than blurting them out. Suggest that the teacher use the blackboard for reminders about schedules and assignments, and also communicate with students by e-mail, or even Facebook.

· 3 ·

Why Context Matters

"Everybody is a genius. But if you judge a fish by its
ability to climb a tree, it will live its whole life believing
that it is stupid."

—Albert Einstein

An Endless Variety of Brains

More than two decades before scientists used magnetic reso-
nance imaging to get a high-tech glimpse of the inside of a human brain, the novelist C. S. Lewis wrote that "what you see and
hear depends a good deal on where you are standing; it also depends on what sort of person you are."

Modern neuroscience has since confirmed this wisdom, establishing that there's simply no such thing as an "average" brain.
Each, instead, provides a unique way of perceiving and reacting
to the world.

It may be hard, and even somewhat unsettling, to accept how
much of your day-to-day experience of a given environment differs from that of others. The vast majority of those differences,

of course, aren't all that meaningful in terms of the impact they have on your life. I think of these differences as *boring* variability. For example, I can roll my tongue—a highly heritable trait. It would be useful for speaking Spanish, if I spoke Spanish. But it's hardly a game-changer in my daily life. Also, and maybe this is a bit less boring, because it's so weird, I actually enjoy the smell of skunk. Go ahead, make fun of me, but the scent takes me back to those mosquito-filled summer evenings as a kid in Hooper, and when experienced in my mind's rearview mirror, at least a little of the chronic misery I felt all through those years dissipates.

The point is that each of us is variable in a startling number of ways, only some of which truly matter in our daily lives. These I call *interesting* variability. Some interesting variability is strongly biological, like my tendencies to be restless and impulsive. Other differences are acquired, such as how our hearing changes as we age. And by this I mean not merely the way older people need you to speak louder, but the way that, past a certain age, we can't hear some sounds altogether, no matter at what volume. This is because most of us, starting in our twenties and thirties (or earlier if you attend too many rock concerts), lose tiny hairs in the inner ear that detect high-frequency noises. Most people who are more than forty years old can't hear anything above 15 kilohertz. (In recent years, some enterprising firms have exploited this difference, selling gadgets that play high-frequency, piercing noise in malls, to shoo away loitering teens. I guess the idea is that if you can hear high frequencies, you probably can't afford to shop.)

Beyond these more obvious differences are others, less visible and more elusive, that matter mightily when it comes to how we learn. Each of us differs, for instance, in the way that we perceive, process, and retain information, in how we organize and express our thoughts, and in the kinds of things that lead us to engage with information or new ideas. Some of these differences have become familiar to us as "disabilities." Unfortunately, this way of thinking has led to a far too narrow, and purely negative, view of variability—a view that ignores the important role of context. Few modern parents, for instance, would be cheered by the news that their child had been diagnosed with dyslexia, a condition affecting perception, which interferes with reading and writing. But what if the story weren't so simple? For instance, what if I told you that, at least in some contexts, neurological differences that are linked to dyslexia can also turn out to be a coveted professional advantage in science?

The Stargazers' Trade-offs

In 2008, I joined a research team at the Harvard-Smithsonian Center for Astrophysics studying a group of talented astrophysicists from all over the world. Based on a theory that we had published about potential visual strengths among people diagnosed with dyslexia, and armed with a grant from the National Science Foundation, we studied a group of astrophysicists, half of them with and half without dyslexia, on a range of tasks that included not only visual and reading measures, but also visual tasks that were central to being an astrophysicist—among them, the detection of black holes. Although preliminary at the time of this writing, the results of the study were interesting, to say the least. Just as we'd hypothesized, the scientists with reading impairments were, as a group, better at detecting black holes than their unimpaired peers.

Our hypothesis about why at least *some* scientists with dyslexia (this isn't, as I'll explain later, a universal advantage) would have this edge had to do with very subtle brain differences, which among other things produce better peripheral vision—not a lot, mind you, but enough to make it interesting. Here's why: As peripheral vision gets better, it can interfere with reading and attention, since it usually makes you more sensitive to distracting stimuli in the environment. And in fact, that's exactly what we saw with our group of scientists. Even as they were seriously impaired in terms of their focused attention and their ability to read, they performed strongly on tasks in which peripheral vision was valuable.

Our study is one of a growing number of scientific attempts to investigate a flip side of a learning "disability." But here's one caveat before we move on: For the purposes of testing our theory, this research involved some extraordinary individuals. Neither my colleagues nor I would go so far as to say that everyone with dyslexia has superior peripheral vision—they don't, because reading is a complex skill, and there will be many ways that someone can be impaired. Nor would we call dyslexia or similar conditions a "gift." That's just as misleading as calling it a "disability," since it ignores the role of context.

To paraphrase Shakespeare, nothing biological is either good or bad, but context makes it so. It's much better, therefore, to think about variability in terms of trade-offs. For most types of variability, in fact, I can imagine at least one context in which it's problematic and one in which it's beneficial. For instance, for most scientists in our study, the differences that made them exceptional in their field were a major source of misery all through school. As I interviewed them, I was repeatedly shocked by the seemingly fresh sorrow of their memories of being punished by teachers who implied they were lazy, and of being bullied and teased by peers. Once their context changed, however, what had seemed a disability became an asset. Our study, therefore, might serve as a reminder of all the potentially underutilized resources we waste when we unilaterally deem differences disabilities. Context matters!

Good News About Novelty-Seeking

A similar "two sides of the same coin" rule applies to another interesting variability, which for me is much closer to home: the chronic, itchy restlessness that goes by the clinical name of "novelty-seeking." The trait is commonly observed in children diagnosed with ADHD and has a strong genetic basis, involving a gene variation (called an allele) that scientists refer to as DRD4-7R. Novelty-seeking goes hand in hand with that low threshold for boredom I told you about in chapter 2. Just as I struggle to stay interested when life turns routine, I'm also way more likely than others I know to be drawn to new experiences. So what does this particular interesting variability mean? Just as in the case of those dyslexic astrophysicists, the answer is: it depends.

Now, psychologists who have made it their business to worry about kids like I used to be have spent considerable time and energy demonstrating the alarming risks of this variability. And it's not as if they lack reasons to fret. Researchers have consistently linked novelty-seeking with risky behaviors including gambling and abuse of drugs and alcohol, to name only a few. Consequently, any well-informed modern parent might reasonably feel some distress to hear that little Johnny or Julie is a "novelty-seeker."

But wouldn't that be a pity? Because the research also clearly shows that novelty-seeking is an important source of curiosity, a trait most parents should want to encourage in their children. Leaving aside what it did to the cat, curiosity has been shown to be a critical component of intelligence, academic and professional success, and healthy relationships, among other virtues and desirable outcomes. One scientific paper called curiosity "the wick in the candle of learning" because of the way it activates the brain's reward system, prompting a burst of dopamine (that neurotransmitter I told you about in chapter 1) to spur the formation of memories. A curious nature represents the same interesting variability, in other words, that could drive a kid to be a heroin addict, a skydiver, or a successful scientist.

So, as we think about novelty-seeking from our complex-systems viewpoint, we realize that of course we should keep a close eye on Johnny's and Julie's choices of after-school activities, especially if he or she is a born risk-taker. Yet we also don't want to ignore or cut off the enormous potential upside of that novelty-seeking trait, which we risk doing when we see it only as a problem. That's how we end up with a mind-set of playing not to lose, rather than playing to win.

I say this as someone who was quite often punished for my curiosity as a child, although never, thank goodness, by my parents, who knew better. As best as I can recall, the first time this happened to me was when I was just ten years old. My Sunday school teacher had just finished explaining to us how God wants us to love everyone, regardless of how "bad" they might be. Even as a kid, this struck me as odd, and since we'd also been told that the Devil was once an angel who had "gone bad," I came up with what I felt was the logical next question: Does that mean we should also love the Devil?

I honestly hadn't intended to provoke my teacher, but he was provoked all the same. He slapped my face, right in front of the rest of the class, saying, "I guess it's no surprise that we can add blasphemy to your list of sins, Todd." For my teacher, my curiosity was nothing less than evil.

That slap may have deterred my curiosity for a while, but about three years later I piped up again, this time inciting the wrath of my eighth-grade algebra teacher. For months in that class I'd been my usual rebellious, low-motivated self, a reliable pain in the neck. But then came an assignment that caught my imagination, as I became fascinated by the idea of a *variable*—the notion that problems could have more than one answer. At home that night, I put aside the formula my teacher had given us to solve our homework problem set and devised my own algorithm, which happened to solve all the problems on our worksheet. I was so thrilled about my discovery that I showed it to my dad, who was talented in math. He agreed that it seemed to work, even though it wasn't a typical approach, and he suggested I show my teacher.

Alas, my teacher didn't share my dad's enthusiasm when I showed him my discovery the following morning.

"It's not right. It doesn't work," he said, shoving the paper aside without a glance in my direction.

I argued that, in fact, it was right—after all, half the answers were provided in the textbook, and the algorithm had worked on them all.

"Todd, go sit down now. It's wrong," he said.

Acting on impulse—again—I refused to walk away. Conscious that my heartbeat was accelerating, I told him, in what I'm sure was a less-than-respectful tone, that he obviously didn't understand math. What had started as a quiet conversation escalated into a shouting match and ended with me sitting in detention. Five minutes after the class ended, my teacher marched into the detention room, approached my desk, and slammed down my worksheet, on which he'd written a new problem, for which my algorithm did not work.

"Don't ever question me in front of my class again," he said, and turned and walked away.

Of course my teacher was right, and I was wrong . . . about the algorithm. But I'd daresay he was terribly wrong about the broader question of how to bring out the best in his students.

Luckily for me, not all my teachers were threatened, or even annoyed by my inquisitiveness. In fact, my best classroom memory from high school is of the encouragement I got in an Advanced Placement history class I managed to enroll in during my sophomore year in high school. (I had begged into the class, not because I loved history, at first, but because I heard the teacher didn't give tests.) My teacher, an expert in the pre-glasnost Soviet Union, routinely reminded us that studying history wasn't about memorizing dates, but rather about probing critically into the complex relationships at play during the time in question to learn why things happened as they did. She loved it when I played the contrarian, asking questions devoid of the knee-jerk Soviet-bashing view so popular at that time. Of course, some of the details are fuzzy, but I clearly remember her smiling response after I followed her lead and connected some dots between a particular food supply problem and a military conflict. She walked over to me and literally shook my hand, saying, "Now that's what it means to think historically!" From that point on, I was hooked, and tried my best—at least in her classroom.

As I moved up the academic food chain, I found that the number of teachers who genuinely appreciated my insistent questioning increased. After all, Albert Einstein himself once said: "I have no special talents; I am only passionately curious." Had no one ever valued this pesky quality of mine, I'm sure I'd never have made my way to Harvard, where today I worry that many bright students are having their curiosity snuffed out at an early age.

What a self-defeating strategy we follow all through grade school! We encourage rigid conformity just when children's brains are most malleable (and most open to exploration) and then try to ignite curiosity and creativity in college and beyond, once so much of the wiring is established. It's a clear sign that we're not thinking seriously enough about the potentially transformative power of context.

Sedentary Nomads

If the case of the dyslexic astrophysicists hasn't fully convinced you of the potentially transformative power of context, consider one more story—this time from the deserts of northern Kenya. Some thirty years ago, while I was suffering away in grade school in Hooper, a large part of a chronically undernourished, cattle-herding tribe known as the Ariaal broke away from their nomadic lifestyle to choose a more settled life as farmers. In 2008, Dan Eisenberg, a first-year graduate student in anthropology at Northwestern University, published his observations of what happened next.

Eisenberg and his collaborators compared a group of 87 settled nomads with 65 who were still wandering with their cattle. They tested them all for DRD4-7R, that gene variant I told you about that's linked to novelty-seeking and other ADHD-like symptoms. Then they logged their body mass, as a measure of nutritional well-being in an environment where food is chronically scarce. They found that the nomads who had the novelty-seeking gene variant, and who had continued their nomadic lives, were on average faring much better than their sedentary cousins with the same genetic quirk.

"Our findings suggest that some of the variety of personalities we see in people is evolutionarily helpful or detrimental, depending on the context," Eisenberg explained, using that word I like so much. "It is possible that in a nomadic setting, a boy with this allele might be able to more effectively defend livestock against raiders or locate food and water sources, but that the same tendencies might not be as beneficial in settled pursuits such as focusing in school, farming, or selling goods." The insight, he added, "might allow us to begin to view ADHD as not just a disease, but something with adaptive components."

It's worth noting that Eisenberg's study neither examined nor explained the precise reasons for the novelty-seeking nomads' comparative good health. Those reasons, moreover, are doubtlessly complex. It could be that the gene variant influenced the nomads' temperament and behavior, making a sedentary life as unhealthy for them as being stuck in a middle school classroom might be for an unusually restless adolescent. Still, Eisenberg cautions that the same hereditary factor is also known to have effects on other parts of the body, including the kidney, meaning that changes in urine excretion, for instance, might be an alternate explanation for the differences in the former nomads' health. Either way, however, the finding offers a vivid argument for the manner in which the same genetic blueprint can end up as a strength or weakness, depending on the context.

For parents and teachers, Eisenberg's research is one more reminder to guide children to environments in which they can shine. You certainly don't need to ship your impertinent questioner off to Kenya, or even sign him up for Outward Bound. But at minimum, please make sure that child isn't being routinely punished for traits that, in the right context and with the right support, could serve as an advantage.

The Evolution of Education

Happily, this big idea—that it's often not so much the kid but the context that sabotages learning—is gaining traction in U.S. education policy. This advancement is due to the work of many individuals and organizations, including two people with whom I've had the honor to collaborate: Anne Meyer and David Rose (no relation), who in 1984 established the nonprofit educational research and development organization called CAST (Center for Applied Special Technology).

Rose is a developmental neuropsychologist and author who also teaches at the Harvard Graduate School of Education. Meyer is a clinical psychologist and educator who studied design and architecture as an undergraduate. The two have long shared a passion for designing learning materials for students with physical and cognitive differences. Their prototype computerized books— some of the first ever created—remain on display at the Smithsonian Museum.

CAST's evolution mirrors recent changes in the way scientists and the public have come to think about the nature of learning abilities and disabilities. It began as a clinic in a hospital, with five employees and fifteen thousand dollars in seed money, but after a few years it moved into its own offices, eventually shedding its medical orientation. Sometime around 1990, as Meyer relates, the CAST team was advancing along in its efforts to create digital books that helped eliminate specific obstacles for kids, when she had an epiphany. "We were working with one student who had a visual disability—so we had to make her buttons talk to her, since she couldn't see them—and another student who could only use his eyes and chin, and then a third who couldn't read very well," Meyer says, "and we said, 'Hey, we're making books for Matt and Megan and Mason. Let's make one book that works for all of them.'"

Meyer came up with the idea of importing to the realm of education a cutting-edge architectural concept known as "universal design," a reference to ways of building structures accessible to all kinds of people, whether they enter in a wheelchair, a stroller, or on their own two feet. "Universal Design for Learning (UDL)" has since entered into policy lexicon as a term for combining new learning sciences research with modern multimedia technology.

Today, CAST's scientists devise ways to support all students, regardless of background or purported disability, primarily by designing environments that represent material in flexible ways and by offering a variety of options for them to demonstrate what they know—going far beyond the standardized test. In practice, the UDL perspective includes both high- and low-tech approaches. It could take shape, for instance, as a software program that lets a second-grade native Spanish-speaker more easily understand a story by reading it on a laptop, with a text-to-speech feature that sounds out new words and provides both images and Spanish translations to define them. Yet it could also include a middle school Mesoamerican history class, whose teacher lets students choose between writing a paper, drawing a poster, or giving a puppet show to demonstrate what they've learned.

Meyer and Rose contend that varying the methods of both teaching and testing will help engage all sorts of kids, not just those identified as "disabled." In other words, they see natural variability as a source of potential innovation, not a problem to be fixed or ignored. A captioned video, for instance, not only helps kids with hearing problems, but also makes life easier for students who are still learning English, or struggling with reading, or merely working in a noisy classroom. The less obvious but equally powerful benefit is that strategies that engage students who were previously tuned out, and therefore prone to disrupt the rest of the class, save precious teacher time previously wasted on crowd management.

CAST today has forty-five employees, working on both research and development and national education policy. Its bookbuilder program, allowing early grade school teachers and students to create their own, free digital books to share with others, has nearly forty thousand users in more than 165 countries, while it is influencing policy from the federal level on down. In a letter to Congress in the fall of 2010, U.S. education secretary Arne Duncan cited UDL as a key facet of the White House's new education strategy, while several states had set up UDL task forces to train teachers and improve curriculum. Harvard Law School dean Martha Minow has called UDL "one of the few big and truly transformative ideas to emerge in education over the past two decades."

This progress has inspired Meyer to envision a day when schools will no longer rely on diagnostic labels, such as dyslexia or ADHD, because children will have options that will eliminate "disabilities" as we know them. The new high- and low-tech supports will increase their access to education just as meaningfully as a wheelchair ramp makes a classroom accessible to someone physically unable to climb stairs—which explains why some activists frame the quest to reshape school environments as a question of civil rights.

"It's His Hair"

Ben Foss, a legal expert, inventor, and policy wonk, is an adamant spokesman for this civil rights perspective on learning differences. As executive director of Disability Rights Advocates, he wages lawsuits to widen access to schools and workplaces for people with all kinds of disabilities.

Foss was diagnosed with dyslexia as a freckled, blue-eyed boy of eight, and bitterly remembers the spelling tests that teachers made him take over and over, and the humiliating "perp walk" to his segregated special-education classes. "The worst part about it is the internalization that you're broken and somehow flawed, and if you just work harder, you'll catch up," he says today.

He didn't speak publicly about his dyslexia until after many years of hard work and private coping strategies that he calls his "secret accommodations" got him admitted to Stanford University's law school. It was there, in 2003, that Foss first read about an Alabama laborer, diagnosed with dyslexia, named Joe Stutts, who struck Foss as the Rosa Parks of the nascent learning disability movement. Stutts had sued his federal government employer in 1983 for having required him to take a written test to get a job operating heavy machinery. His courage inspired Foss to form an education and pressure group for people with dyslexia, which he called Headstrong Nation.

Three years later, having temporarily sidelined his legal career, Foss got a new job in the venture capital unit of Intel, where he serendipitously entered the ranks of UDL inventors. While sitting in his cubicle one day, he started playing with his cell phone and realized, as he recalls, "that I could take a picture and send it to my computer and have the computer do optical recognition and turn it into text and have it read aloud to me." Intel helped him develop the gizmo, which was dubbed the Intel Reader, betting that it would be popular not only with people with dyslexia, but with a growing market of aging baby boomers whose weakening eyesight makes it hard to read small print. (The Reader can also adjust font size.) Foss takes pride in his invention, even as it still nags at him that it was reviewed by the online magazine *Engadget* as a tool "for the lazy and infirm." On reading this, he says, "at first I thought, 'Oh, no!,' and then I realized I was grateful that they'd actually written down the bias."

Foss's combative spirit dates back to his childhood, during which it was his good luck to have exceptionally understanding parents. His mother, Susan Moore, had served in the Peace Corps in Nigeria, and applied her worldly imagination to her parenting. "I figured it was less important how my kids were doing in school than whether they were actually learning," she says.

Moore adopted several conventionally smart parenting strategies, such as educating herself about dyslexia, while encouraging Foss to take up soccer and energetically applauding any of his school triumphs, taping the best of his drawings on the refrigerator. As my own mom did, she also frequently followed her gut, even when others couldn't understand.

Foss likes to tell about the time when he was four and his

mother took him for a haircut. After seating him in the chair, the stylist asked what kind of cut he wanted. Foss said he didn't want his hair cut at all. His mother promptly tipped the stylist, and started to walk out the door with her son. "You're going to let a four-year-old tell you what to do?" the man sputtered.

"It's his hair" was Moore's reply.

Several years later, while Foss was enduring his worst times in school, Moore made an even more unusual decision: She began letting him trash his room on the many afternoons that he returned home in a rage at his teachers.

"At first, I wasn't sure if I was doing the right thing," Moore recalls. "But he was very frustrated, and I thought he had so much anger in him that it would be better to get it out than have it stewing."

Foss remembers: "I'd pull my bookcase over, smash my audio-tapes, and once even threw my boom box out the window. My mom and I made a deal that I could destroy anything in my room, but the catch was that I had to deal with the consequences."

Once again, Moore allowed Foss an unusual degree of autonomy, with an equal amount of responsibility. From the perspective of complex systems, her mothering tactics were pure genius. By allowing her son to vent his anger, she short-circuited a cycle that could easily have sabotaged Foss, had his rage built to the point that he took it out on people at school. At the same time, however, she taught him the value of self-control by making him responsible for his actions.

The approach has become a keystone of Foss's philosophy of education. "What is education really for?" he asks. "It shouldn't be to make you behave and be obedient. It's to help you do what you want." Moreover, while Foss thinks of education as a fundamental right, he considers it the student's responsibility to understand his or her strengths and weaknesses and find the supports that will lead to independence.

Luckily, such supports are becoming increasingly common—and less stigmatized—in schools throughout the United States. Change has come slowly, however, and even today, far too many kids are getting the message, all day and every day, that they are broken, useless, and unwanted.

BIG IDEAS
● ▪ ● ▪ ● ▪ ● ▪ ●

- There is no such thing as an average brain. Variability is the rule, not the exception.
- Some of this "interesting" variability directly influences the ability to learn, making a compelling case for designing flexible environments that deal effectively with these differences.
- A preference for novelty is a genetic variability that at its worst can contribute to negative outcomes such as gambling and drug and alcohol abuse. At its best, the trait can serve as the basis for curiosity, a characteristic essential to achievement and happiness. The choice between these outcomes will, among other things, depend on a child's context.
- Education policy experts have been reaching a consensus that it's more important to focus efforts to change school environments than to try to change the natural variability of our children.

ACTION ITEMS
● ■ ● ■ ● ■ ● ■ ● ■ ● ■ ●

- To most effectively help your square-peg child, start by understanding your own "interesting" variability, and how it influences your relationships and is influenced by varying contexts.
- Remember to add nuance to your curiosity about your children's behavior. Rather than ask why your child behaved in a certain way, ask why he or she behaved that way *in that context*.
- Think about how your child's variability plays out in different contexts. Identify at least one context where your child usually excels and another where he or she struggles.

▪ 4 ▪

Ostracized

"Be kind, for everyone you meet is fighting a hard battle."
—PLATO

A Good Day Is When Bad Things Don't Happen

"YOU ARE A BITCH!"

It was the first time I'd ever heard my mom curse. She yelled the words into the telephone receiver and promptly slammed it down.

Naturally, I had to see what the problem was—frankly, less out of concern for my mother's emotional state and more to look for clues as to what kind of punishment was coming my way.

I crept up the stairs from my bedroom in the basement and stuck my head around the door to get a glimpse inside the kitchen. After hearing the commotion, my dad had come into the room from the garage. He put his arm around my mother as she leaned on the linoleum counter, looking more miserable than I had ever seen her.

At the ripe old age of ten, I was already used to being the bad guy, guilty or not, so I naturally assumed that I was the cause of whatever had made her that angry. I could only just make out her words, as she murmured, "Well, I guess I lost another friend."

Squinting, I tried to remember: What could I have done, now? Or, rather, what had they found out?

I didn't have long to puzzle it over. My dad caught sight of me on the stairs, just as I was trying to slide back down. My mom turned her head to follow his gaze, and to my surprise, walked over and hugged me, weeping anew, and saying, "I'm so sorry."

Eventually, she told me what had happened. Her now former best friend, Peggy, had called to inform her that she would be breaking a longtime tradition of our small town, which was that whenever any child had a birthday party, every kid of that age was invited. "Nobody wants Todd at the party," Peggy had said. "He will ruin it."

She wasn't entirely wrong about that. I've already mentioned my little problem with impulsivity, and back then, especially, parties reliably revved me up. I was famous for doing things like blowing out candles on other kids' birthday cakes, or blurting out the contents of a present before it was opened, and pounding other kids on their backs in what always seemed to me like a hearty greeting, but which some kids claimed actually hurt them. Many times, after I left a playmate's house, coveted toys would be missing. Eventually, people of all ages took to cringing when they saw me show up at social events. At twelve, as I ran through the front door of the church social hall, to attend the bishop's wife's fancy "etiquette dinner" to teach us kids some table manners, the hostess literally grabbed me by the collar as if she were a mafia thug and pushed me up against the wall, hissing, "You are not going to ruin this for me, do you understand, Todd?"

As best I can recall, she succeeded in scaring me straight—for that night. But within days I was back in trouble again. I had so few friends that I would do just about anything to get attention, which of course nearly always backfired. At the annual performance by my middle school choir, I scrambled onstage just before the curtain went up to join four preselected soloists. I hadn't been preselected, because I couldn't sing, a deficit all of my choir-mates had witnessed. "What are you doing?" the kid next to me whispered as the curtain went up. "Mr. Harkness tapped me to go!" I lied. We continued to argue until the song began. I mouthed my way through it, and basked briefly in the undeserved applause. In later years, my bids for attention escalated to so reckless a degree that when Hooper's old church building burned to the ground one night, my dad braced for the worst, until he heard that someone else's kids had done it. Then he grinned, exclaiming, "Let's get those brats!"

Adolescence is hard for most kids, but for naturally impulsive, socially awkward square pegs it can be a nonstop nightmare. It's the time when the world's expectations increase and you reliably disappoint. The consequence for all too many children is that former relationships fall apart just when they need them the most.

Sam Goldstein, the psychologist who evaluated me at sixteen, once said something I've always remembered: "A good day for challenging kids is when bad things don't happen." By the time I was ten, my mother could see that I'd lost every single one of my former friends and cost her several of her own. But there was much more she didn't know, at least for many years thereafter, mainly because I was too mortified to tell her.

Worse than Ostracized

Chief among these private mortifications was how I spent my lunch hours all through middle school. Halfway through seventh grade, that particularly eventful, awful year, I'd stopped trying to sit with other kids, after some of them threw food at me to make me go away. I was so embarrassed about having to sit all by myself that I repeatedly broke one of the strictest school rules by sneaking off campus to spend my lunch hours playing video games in the nearby community recreation center. The vice principal caught me about as often as he didn't, and I wound up with a string of detentions. But this was no deterrent, since the alternative of facing that teasing all alone was so much worse. What's more, in detention I'd always have company for lunch.

My mom also stayed in the dark about Casey, the ninth grader who used to beat me up almost every day after school. I never understood his reasons for this. I can't recall that I'd ever crossed him personally, so ultimately I figured it could only have been because I'd been marked as a loser, low down in the schoolyard pecking order, incredibly annoying and all but defenseless, so that it was easy for other kids who were unsure about their own status to score some points at my expense.

Every afternoon, Casey rode the bus with me home from school, and time after time, would get off at my stop instead of his and chase me down the street. My house was only about three hundred yards from the stop, yet even though I always made sure to sit up in front of the bus, so I'd have that much more of a head start, I never once managed to outrun him. At some point he would always catch up, tackle me, and then, as I lay on the ground, slug and kick me a few times, after which he'd spit on me and walk away. The routine never varied; it was almost like he saw it as his job.

Those beatings hurt a lot, but what was far worse was the way no one ever came to my defense. On the contrary: Kids would lean out the bus windows to get a good view. The bus driver also watched, yet not once did she intervene—even after I summoned the nerve one day to complain to her. She was probably glad to see me get my comeuppance; in truth I'd been annoying her for months, shouting, throwing paper airplanes, and opening windows she'd ordered us to keep closed.

Had my mom known that any of this was going on, she would surely have gone after Casey and the bus driver to boot. But I couldn't stand the thought of her finding out. It made me feel queasy to think of her seeing how far I'd fallen. I could almost pretend it wasn't happening if I kept it secret from her. She was always telling me how good-looking she thought I was, and how much potential I had to do great things, so perhaps I also thought that if she knew the full extent of how much people didn't like me, she might be swayed to revise her opinion.

And so, after every beating, I'd either run into the back of our garage and clean myself off with my father's grease rags or, if that weren't possible, invent some excuse for why my shirt was torn or my lip was split. I remember stumbling into our house, crying, and saying I'd fallen down while playing. More than two decades later, after I finally told her the truth, my mom was furious with me for keeping it a secret for so long.

My mom feels guilty that she didn't stop the bullying, yet I have never blamed her for not knowing what was going on. I reserve that blame for my school. Kids are kids, and it wouldn't be realistic to think that schools could completely eliminate occasional teasing and bullying. But no school employee—including bus drivers—should ignore signs that a child is being systematically victimized.

Given all we've learned about bullying in the intervening years—including how prevalent, and often secretive, it is, and its uniquely devastating impact, both on the brain and on behavior—I am heartened that schools are finally starting to focus harder on this problem, although I believe they should also be doing much more. In recent surveys, one-third of U.S. schoolchildren—an estimated 13 million students—have reported being teased and bullied at school, with more than one in ten of these suffering physical abuse, such as being shoved, spit on, and tripped. Addressing the problem head-on would be more than simply compassionate. From someone with direct experience of the costs, I can assure you that bullying wastes time and money throughout our education system, and there is no question that it sabotages learning.

Bullying Dumbs You Down

Education experts have been sounding alarms about bullying for several years now, and, to be sure, many conscientious school directors have worked hard in various ways to curtail it. Only quite recently, however, has there been serious momentum for change.

In March 2011, a few weeks after a highly publicized wave of half a dozen suicides of adolescent boys who'd been persecuted at school or over the Internet, President Barack Obama presided over the first White House conference dedicated to combating bullying. Obama, who revealed that he himself had been bullied and teased as a child, said his goal was to "dispel the myth that bullying is just a harmless rite of passage or an inevitable part of growing up."

Indeed, a great deal of recent research has detailed the lasting harm that bullying causes its victims—and the most effective measures that schools can take to prevent it. (I'll talk more about this in chapter 6.) Sadly, the research also makes clear that my seventh-grade torment was typical, at least in some ways, to what happens every day to millions of American students.

For one thing, I got bullied in middle school, where bullying is most common: More than 40 percent of the reported cases involve kids in grades six through eight, compared to less than half that in elementary and high school. As a boy, I was also more likely to be bullied than if I'd been a girl—and as a boy with learning struggles and poor self-esteem, even more so.

It wasn't the least bit exceptional, moreover, that my mistreatment was chronic. About one in five victims say they get teased or bullied once or twice a month, while one in ten get bullied several times a week or even daily. Nor was it unusual that I kept quiet. One-third of the victims in surveys said they've never reported the bullying at school. Instead they often tune out and shut down.

Rather than admit they're being bullied, many children will simply pretend to be sick or find other excuses to avoid school. As many as 160,000 students miss school each day in the United States for fear of being bullied, according to the National Association of School Psychologists. Dash Seerley Gowland, a middle schooler who was diagnosed with ADHD and teased almost every day in and out of class, described the experience in a letter he wrote to his mother. "I wake up and my stomach lurches like a mad 'eel' because I hate school," he wrote. "I dread school so much . . . that I try to make myself barf so much that I won't have to go to school. But my mother sees right through me. Even though she feels my pain, like having a knife stabbed into her, she makes me go anyhow."

Just as Gowland's imagery suggests, the pain of social rejection is in many ways on par with physical suffering, both for lonely kids and their empathetic mothers. Neuroscientists have shown that both types of pain activate the same brain regions, specifically the secondary somatosensory cortex and the dorsal posterior insula. While of course being teased is not the same as being stabbed with a knife, it's surprising how similarly the brain treats the two. And it makes me wonder: if a child came home from school with what we now know are the neural equivalents of knife wounds, would we really want to tell him to suck it up and get back to business?

My life improved after my nemesis, Casey, turned sixteen, got his driver's license, and stopped taking my bus. Yet throughout the next two years, I had a nightmare that evoked the same feeling I had when he was chasing me down the street. It went like this: I'd be sitting alone in a rowboat on Bear Lake, a vacation spot near Idaho where my family vacationed each year, when all of a sudden the winds would whip up waves as tall as skyscrapers. I knew I'd done something wrong to land me in that boat but didn't know what it was, or how to save myself. I could see a lighthouse in the distance, but each time I turned my eyes toward it, my rowboat would shrink. Night after night, my boat became steadily smaller until I felt the waves pulling me under, and I'd wake up, dripping in sweat.

As I understand today, my problem, likely shared with Dash Gowland and many others, was that my fear had worked its way into my very bloodstream, in the form of (among other things) a chemical called cortisol. Cortisol surges in the body and brain when we perceive a threat. Its purpose is an all-hands-on-deck mustering of energy to get a mammal moving quickly, to flee or to fight. It's a kind of triage system that takes place at the expense of the normal maintenance functions that happen when a body is at rest—like calling away plumbers and cleaners at a hospital to help carry stretchers.

For most mammals, the system works quite well. "For 99 percent of the beasts on this planet, stress is about three minutes of screaming terror," says the Stanford stress scientist Robert Sapolsky, "after which it's either over with or you're over with." Yet the problem for the remaining one percent, in other words, modern humans, is that we have the unique ability to worry about the future, like what fresh hell will Casey dish out tomorrow? Under repeated stress, pretty soon, the cortisol is flowing several times a day, day after day, and month after month, until, as Sapolsky's research has shown, the body's normal maintenance operations break down. In a particularly terrible irony for kids who already have learning problems, part of the damage is that cells in a brain structure called the hippocampus, critical to memory, shrivel up and die.

This is what I mean when I say bullying dumbs you down.

The effects are not only pernicious over time, but they are obvious in the moment. When reacting to a threat, a person who might normally test about average for working memory can shoot down as far as the second percentile (where I've staked my claim). It's that big an impact. Learning is simply not a priority during those moments of "screaming terror," so every part of the brain that might help it along essentially shuts down. Curiosity takes a backseat, as do judgment and self-control. What makes this story all the more heartbreaking is that a kid who is already a target for bullying and punishment because of his behavior will likely end up behaving even worse when he's under constant threat, which in turn makes him even more of a target. Similar to what happens when children get physically punished by their parents, this is a classic example of how negative feedback loops can create a downward spiral that reliably ends in some crisis, such as drug addiction, a suicide attempt, or the victim turning into a victimizer.

While a large proportion of victims—and, notably, also bullies—suffer from anxiety and depression, many develop characteristics that attract much less sympathy. They can get defensive, irritable, and argumentative, overreacting to the slightest or even an imaginary provocation. In many cases, this might lead to a diagnosis of oppositional defiant disorder, or ODD. As many as 60 percent of kids diagnosed with ADHD also qualify for this particularly controversial diagnosis, research suggests. Among its "symptoms," as listed in the *Diagnostic and Statistical Manual of Mental Disorders,* the atlas of psychiatry, are "frequent temper tantrums," "excessive arguing with adults," "questioning rules," and "blaming others for his or her mistakes or behavior."

As I've mentioned before, while I remain deeply skeptical about the value of labels from a scientific standpoint, I also recognize that, practically speaking, some diagnostic labels may be helpful, at least at the start of a parent's or teacher's journey to help a child. But let me be blunt: The fact that we are pinning a label of ODD on so many kids makes me, well, pretty irritable and argumentative. It suggests that 100 percent of the blame for a child's behavior belongs to that child, when it's also likely that child is essentially reacting reasonably to years of hostile treatment. In particular, I see "questioning rules" less as a symptom of pathology than a trait I'd like to encourage in my students.

What's missing when the ODD label is slapped over a label of ADHD, or dyslexia, or whatever, is any insight into the reasons why such kids are behaving the way that they are—in particular, it's ignorant of the interactions between biology and context that led up to, and the feedback loops that sustain, the bad behavior. It presents the child as a patient with a biological glitch that needs "fixing," as if he or she had been born with a contentious nature, rather than, as is usually more likely, building up the opposition over time. And it ignores all that we now know about how living under threat, and being routinely swamped by cortisol, can damage the brain.

Faking It

By the time I got to middle school, my mom understood that I was not exactly a social magnet. Even so, I took pains to hide the extent of my suffering from her and anyone else who showed

interest, even when that meant I had to lie, and mostly, I succeeded. The psychologist Sam Goldstein's notes from my office
visit during my junior year in high school say, "Todd seeks out
and is sought out by peers for friendship," a statement that, sadly,
was pure fiction. Short of trailing me around school himself, however, Goldstein was obliged to rely on my own reports and my
parents' limited observations. Knowing this, I put a big smiley
face on my miserable life, even inventing a "best friend"—citing
the name of a kid who would have been shocked to hear himself
described that way.

Even as I remember those fables I told, I'm surprised today by
the level of detail in Goldstein's report, which dwells attentively
on my earliest years, even as it makes no mention of how much
trouble I was getting into at school. True, Goldstein cited com-
plaints by three of my teachers about my restlessness and distractibility, yet from reading his report, one wouldn't get any idea
of all the time I spent in detention, nor of the overall, abject
misery of my daily life.

Rather than being "sought out" for friendship, I remember
burning up with jealousy of a kid my age named Stephan, who
for reasons I can't remember today was confined to a wheelchair.
Because of his obvious disability, the same, popular kids who
enjoyed tormenting me made a point of showing what good people they were by including him in their group, and even taking
turns pushing his chair around the campus. I used to dream about
trading places with him.

Was there anything, really, that Goldstein or my mother could
have done to make me open up and share that gloomy vision?
Honestly, I doubt it. And so, the only advice I might now offer

my mother, were I able to travel back in time and whisper in her ear, would be to assume that what she already knew of my struggles at school was merely the tip of a cold, lonely iceberg. She didn't have much power to change things for me at that point. We couldn't afford a private school, and even my feisty, energetic mom couldn't have forced kids at my public school to be kind to me.

All she could do was to try to understand me, a job I know I made ever more difficult for her as my misery increased. To this day, I feel crummy, for instance, about how nasty I was to my family through those years. I wish I could change that, since they are such a wonderful part of my life now. All I can say in my defense is that back then I had experienced so little empathy from other people that I wasn't yet capable of showing it. Moreover, in a world in which I felt I spent much of my time preparing for and weathering attacks, empathy wasn't a useful trait. It seemed then that my choice boiled down to being bullied or bullying. I chose, as I saw it, to avoid being a victim.

Gravitating to a group of other misfits, I took out my anger on strangers. We smashed mailboxes with baseball bats, and once or twice threw lit firecrackers at passing cars. Once, under cover of darkness, we dropped a makeshift scarecrow—a pumpkin head, and shirts and pants, all stuffed with tomatoes—in front of a car passing under a tree that overhung the road. (There were no streetlights, and the sudden impact so frightened the poor driver that he jumped out of his car screaming, worried that he'd injured or even killed someone.) I stole cash from a neighbor's house when no one was home, and for a short time even sold fake IDs I helped produce with a friend who had a color printer and plastic casings I swiped from the DMV. (Because I had no formal income at the time, I ended up using the substantial proceeds—the IDs sold for a hundred dollars apiece—to take my friends out to breakfast.)

These were all obviously more than your average high school high jinks. It was no more than luck, many times, that kept me out of juvenile hall, and the memories of the risks I took with other people's safety and my own still distress me, two decades later. I can't offer any excuse for that behavior, only an explanation: At some point I got trapped in one of those negative feedback loops, or more like an out-of-control downward spiral.

My dad, as I see now, was trapped right along with me in that spiral. He'd punish me, and I would hurt others, or mouth off to teachers or my mom, after which he'd punish me more, and so on. Now let me be clear, I'm not saying he was the cause of my behavior (he wasn't), and I sympathize with how he must have felt at that time. Angry and scared that I was headed for jail or worse, he tried desperately to stop it the only way he knew how—with ever-stricter punishments, which drove me ever further away from him.

Our brawling also created a rift between my parents. My dad accused my mom of not being tough enough, of coddling me and being too quick with excuses for me. In fact, however, my mom was often even angrier over my behavior than my dad was. Still, at this critical time in my life, when it looked like the world was caving in on me, she recognized that someone had to detach and deescalate instead of engaging and amplifying the negative feedback loops.

We usually assume that parenting is one-directional. Parents influence their children, not vice versa. But Lyda's personality was transformed through the crucible of my adolescence, when, as the hands-on parent while my dad was usually at work or school, she had to evolve to survive. Educating herself about the way my brain worked, and thereby understanding better how her own brain worked, made her more self-aware, improving her control over her own reactions. My father, to his credit, would make the same progress in time, but at a distance, and not forged by that same fire.

The depth of the way Lyda was changing became clear on the night she swore at her friend Peggy. As she'd tell me years later, she'd come to believe that, despite my tough-guy act, I desperately needed at least one person uncompromisingly on my side, and that if she didn't step in at that point, no one would. She let me know that, if it came to it, she'd choose me over any of her friends if they persisted in characterizing me as hopelessly bad.

And she went on, from that day, taking stands for me—not ever to excuse my terrible behavior (the worst of which, thank goodness, never reached her ears at that time), but letting the world know that she, at least, was in my corner. One tactic I've come to appreciate in particular is that she'd often suspend a punishment she'd planned for me (and which I usually deserved) if she saw that I had already gotten my comeuppance elsewhere. At the time, she figured that I could only take so much negative input before I'd start to shut down, a philosophy that starts to look like genius when you consider all we've learned about the pernicious effects that sustained high cortisol levels have on the brain.

"I didn't want to be blind to the fact that you were obnoxious and irritating to people," my mom told me many years later, with her usual dearth of diplomacy. "So I had to learn how to pick my battles. It was okay that someone didn't love or even like you. Sometimes it was difficult for *me*, too. But attack you—watch out!"

Islands of Competence—and the Magic of Spandex

In time, it became one of my greatest (albeit mostly secret) joys to watch Lyda go on the warpath on my behalf. My high school teachers and the lay church leaders all learned not to cross her. She'd reliably call and chew them out after any incidents like the time my fashion-impaired Sunday school teacher made fun of me for wearing a black linen jacket with the sleeves pushed up (à la Crockett, the super-cool *Miami Vice* TV detective) to church. I was by then taking clothes so seriously that I'd save up for months to buy a pair of designer jeans, trusting that other kids would be in awe at least of my fashion sense. In this case, however, it was my mom who'd saved up to buy the linen jacket for me, which made her all the more incensed at that Sunday school teacher.

At the same time, Lyda kept her eyes out for opportunities where I'd have a chance to genuinely feel competent, and maybe even shine a little. She seemed at least as delighted as I was when I made the high school basketball team in tenth grade, and she was there at every game that I ever played in—even better, she'd routinely stay out with me late at night, many nights, rebounding missed shots from the hoop in our driveway. When my grades got so bad that school administrators tried to take me off the team, she came to my defense, even summoning my pediatrician as a witness, arguing that my meager emotional investment in school was sure to disappear if I lost this key incentive.

Today, I picture my mother's efforts as having helped me to build what psychologist Bob Brooks calls "islands of competence"— little strongholds where I could feel safe and somewhat in control, and where I could anchor my self-esteem. It didn't matter whether she shared the same interests with me—in fact, she always reminded me that it was my life, and I should find things that I enjoyed. She figured the type of pursuits I chose—as long as they were legal—were less important than the fact that I had chosen them and that they gave me an opportunity to feel competent. I have often since talked to parents who've nudged their square-peg children away from activities that seemed to them (the parents) like a waste of time. My feeling is that whether your child takes pride in being a good chess player, a collector of rocks, or even in being the best Call of Duty player on his block, the value-add is going to be the same. It's about feeling pride for something that you've done, and done well. And, most likely, it's a rare and precious feeling for that child.

Something else that my mother clearly understood is that these little islands of competence, such as my basketball prowess, should never be used as bargaining chips. This can be difficult, I know, since parents naturally want to exploit any incentive available to get a child to improve his behavior. And the tactic may work with most kids. Still, it's almost certain to backfire when a child needs any authentic positive attention he can get to build up his flagging self-esteem. These islands are refuges amid stormy waters, and they also represent ideal places for lonely kids to make friends with other kids who share the same interests. If you take away their one reason to think well of themselves, why shouldn't they just stop trying?

When others, including my dad, charged Lyda with spoiling me, her wise reaction was to seek out allies who shared her out-of-the-box approaches. Parents of challenging kids need strong emotional support, and often, fortunately, it's there for the asking, although not nearly as much as it should be. Lyda gathered a small team of stalwarts who sided with her for siding with me. They included one of her sisters, a friend who was a practicing psychologist, and, most important, her mother, Grandma Burton.

Studies on why certain children are resilient while others crumble at bad turns of fate have repeatedly found one constant: a relationship with at least one adult other than a parent who gives the child unconditional love. All through my entire childhood, my grandma fulfilled that role, showing an almost mystical knack for knowing when I needed her most. Some of my best childhood memories are of the times when I slept over at her house. Most of these nights, as I now understand, were times when my parents desperately needed a break.

Our routine rarely varied: We'd go to Sizzler for a cheap steak, and then stay up late playing games such as Yahtzee and Aggravation for hours at a time. Unlike almost every other adult in my life, my grandma showed no interest whatsoever in trying to fix me, or change me, or even talk to me about how I was doing in school. Instead she'd praise my fledgling sense of humor, even as she taught me about comic timing, and the thin line between wit and sarcasm. I was so keen to make other people laugh, and in particular to win my grandmother's approval, that under her patient tutelage, this became one of the few areas of my life where I started to practice self-restraint.

My grandmother's own sense of timing was exquisite, and not just with humor. She unfailingly seized opportunities to show me I was loved. There was the time, for instance, when I was about eleven years old, and, running past a table, accidentally knocked over a vintage Avon cologne bottle that was in the shape of a car and that she had repeatedly asked me not to touch. It was important to my grandmother—precious, actually—because she had taken it from her father's house when he passed away. It was one of the very few mementos that she had left. I figured she'd be furious. It seemed like I was always breaking other people's things, I was so clumsy. I barely dared to look at her as she was sweeping up the pieces, but when she finally caught my eye, all she said was "People are more important than things."

It was only years later that she admitted to me how upset she was about that broken bottle. At the time, however, my grandma was thinking strategically. She recognized that the loss was also an opportunity for her to prove that I was important to her, and she took full advantage of it.

Grandma Burton, alas, would have many other chances to restrain herself from overreacting to all the trouble I caused, but the one for which I'm most thankful came after my seventh-grade stink bomb debacle. My poor mom was so thrown by this behavior, which was so much worse than my usual impulsivity, that she stopped talking to me altogether for the entire day. My dad also gave me the silent treatment. I remember sitting alone in my room, feeling sure that I'd finally pushed them both too far, wondering if they were ready to abandon me, like my great-grandparents did to my grandpa, and if I'd have to go live in a junkyard.

I heard a knock on my door, and before I could answer, my grandma walked in, with a white box wrapped in ribbon. She wasn't smiling, but she did look straight in my eyes as she sat on my bed and handed me the gift, which turned out to be a pair of Spandex shorts, an ultrafashionable (for Hooper, Utah, circa 1987) style that I'd coveted for months, but which I knew my parents couldn't afford. (Nor could my grandmother, a fact that wasn't lost on me.)

"It is not because I'm proud of what you did. It's because I love you," was all she said.

As I've said before in these pages, I can't really credit any one moment or person for helping me change, although of course I owe the largest debt to my mom. Still, I know my grandma's gift could not have been more timely or important. I am quite sure it would be hard to find a psychologist or child-rearing "expert" who would prescribe such a gift at such a time. I suspect most experts would even disparage her decision, claiming she was unintentionally rewarding me for my aggressive behavior. Luckily for me, she didn't consult specialists. Instead she trusted her instincts, which told her to go ahead and show me I was still worthy of love.

BIG IDEAS
● ▪ ● ▪ ● ▪ ▪ ● ▪ ●

- An estimated 13 million U.S. children get bullied and teased every year, with 1.3 million suffering physical abuse.

- Bullying is most common in middle school, involves boys more often than girls, and often goes on for a long time without being reported.

- The stress hormone cortisol floods the brain and body when someone feels threatened, and over the long term having too much of it in your system for too long can damage parts of the brain essential for memory and attention.

- The diagnosis of oppositional defiant disorder, applicable to as many as 60 percent of children diagnosed with ADHD, is likely less a medical condition than a result of a damaging, out-of-control feedback loop, in which a child is lashing out against his environment after possibly years of negative reactions. It is not a satisfying explanation for any child's emotional struggles.

- Getting sent to detention in the morning means you'll at least have company for lunch.

ACTION ITEMS

- Look for authentic opportunities to "take a stand" for your child—when he or she has been poorly treated, it matters less what you say than what you do to show your support.
- When your child or student seems socially isolated, irritable, and reluctant to go to school, spend at least as much time investigating the quality of his or her environment as you do in seeking a diagnosis.
- Don't just correct the negative. Add positive influences to your child's environment. Help build "islands of competence" and do your best to protect them. If all your son and daughter have to look forward to is a basketball game or school play, don't take that away as a punishment.
- Every square-peg child should have at least one adult outside the immediate family who provides appreciation and support. Do what you can to make sure your child has such an adult in his or her life, including letting people know the role that they might play to help—you'd be surprised how many aunts or uncles will be happy to be the "good cop."

Fitting In—and Dropping Out

"Play the part and you shall become."

—UNKNOWN

What Would Jimmy Do?

By my sophomore year in high school, my grades were rock-bottom and my social status even lower. I still didn't have a single close friend, and girls outright ignored me when they weren't making fun of me. I'd attended just one of the school dances, and only had a date that night because the girl's mother had pressured her to do the right thing. (She'd hoped to go with another boy, but I'd asked her first.) I was miserable, and made sure the rest of my family was, too, by constantly picking fights with my mom and my siblings.

Still, a few weeks before my seventeenth birthday, a constellation of events that had little to do with me, specifically, ended up changing my context, which, in turn, changed me.

While I'd been slogging through grades six through ten, my dad had been busy with his own ambitious agenda. For several years, he'd been working at a truck repair shop by day and taking college engineering classes at night. Out of the blue one morning, or so it seemed to me, he informed us that he'd gotten a new job at an airbag-manufacturing company called Autoliv. Our family would be leaving rural Hooper for Layton, just fourteen miles away, and a comparatively booming metropolis, with its population of fifty-eight thousand. My dad's new salary would pay for a much nicer house for us, and I'd be going to a new school.

While many kids my age might have protested being uprooted from their social circles, I was unambiguously overjoyed. I recognized that this was my chance to try to reinvent myself with a whole new group of peers. And by this, I didn't mean academically. Improving my grades was not my priority, as my report cards from Layton would soon show. The first item on my agenda was no longer to be teased, slugged, and spit on by schoolmates. Next, I wanted some new friends. If it seems at all hard to understand that I'd put friends before scholastic success that might guarantee me a brighter future, I'll merely point out that the only kinds of people I've ever heard claim that academics are more important than friends are people who already have friends. If you're as isolated as I was then, nothing else matters.

I can't say that I plotted my course at my new high school with strategic brilliance, since all I really knew at that point was what *didn't* work. As it turned out, however, that was enough. Today, I compare my situation to the classic episode of *Seinfeld* in which Seinfeld tells his feckless friend George, "if every instinct you have is wrong, then the opposite would have to be right." George agrees, and promptly starts doing the opposite of everything he has done in the past, from ordering something completely different for lunch to being frank with a beautiful woman he meets, revealing that he's unemployed and lives with his parents. To his joyful surprise, the "Opposite George" tactic gets him dates.

In a similar spirit, I resolved to be "Opposite Todd." I had a general sense of the kinds of things I'd been doing to put people off. I stood too close, bragged too much, interrupted a lot, and always seemed to say the wrong thing. I didn't understand how to fix any one of these problems. Yet I sensed I could make progress by patterning myself after someone completely unlike me who was obviously doing everything right. My model turned out to be a kid named Jimmy, who was the quarterback of the football team at the high school I was leaving. Jimmy was such a nice guy that he had occasionally even let me follow him around. From my first day at Layton High, in every social encounter, I'd simply ask myself, "What would Jimmy do?"

Mimicking Jimmy educated me. It showed me, for one thing, how I was unconsciously contributing to many of the negative feedback loops that had made life miserable for me—pushing people away even in the way I greeted them. "What's up, dick?" had been my customary salutation. I thought it was funny, and, besides, from my perspective, this was how people always talked to me. But Jimmy never talked like that to anyone, no matter how high or low they ranked socially. Instead he'd say things like "What's up, stud?" and always be greeted with a smile. From the first time I tried this at Layton High, I got the same result, which brought a revelation: People like to be complimented! And so the insights emerged, until soon I seemed even to myself to be turning into a different person. A person other kids actually liked.

It wasn't exactly gratifying to think that I needed to become another person to be accepted. When you're growing up, everyone tells you, "Just be yourself!" So at first, copying Jimmy seemed like I'd accepted that I could never be liked for myself. Only later did I recognize that I wasn't really changing who I was, but merely abandoning ways of behaving that had backfired for me for years.

Besides, it's hard to argue with success. Especially when you look around one day, as I did, and realize you're sitting at the apex of teenage social status.

Alpha Male

The inner sanctum of juvenile prestige at Layton High was an otherwise ordinary row of carpeted stairs set against a wall in an indoor hallway in the middle of campus. Set off by two pillars, the area was known as the Commons, and it was understood throughout the school that if you didn't fit in, you couldn't hang out there. Most kids would detour around those pillars rather than walk through them, while the elite group that I was so delighted to have joined sat or stood on the stairs. We looked like a Nordstrom back-to-school ad, the girls in their cheerleader skirts and the boys in our Girbaud jeans and sports jerseys, emitting a faint cloud of sweat and cheap cologne.

A couple of burly members of our crowd kept an eye out for any outsider so clueless as to trespass on our privileged real estate. The fiercest of these watchmen was a talented basketball player and chronic troublemaker named Blake, who also happened to be one of my new friends. We had started playing basketball after school, and as point guard—and once again following a strategy I'd learned from Jimmy—I'd pass to him as often as I could, rather than hogging the ball, as I'd always done before then. Blake appreciated that, and we hit it off. Given that Blake's loyalty was as fierce as his appearance, I could relax in the knowledge that my days of being bullied were over.

With my safety assured, I could finally focus on getting some dates, and this, too, turned out to be surprisingly easy. Within my first three weeks at Layton High, I was going out with two of the most sought-after girls in the school. Sandra and Mary were both in my chemistry class, where I not only hadn't thrown any stink bombs that year, but had charmed both the teacher and my fellow students. Sandra already had a boyfriend, who threatened to beat me up after I took her to a Utah Jazz basketball game. But he backed off after I stood up to him.

Hmmm. Stood up to him? Okay, that's not *quite* what happened. Frankly, I froze in fear when he approached me and threatened to kick my teeth in if I didn't stop seeing his girlfriend. The truth is that I wanted to run away, but I couldn't. My feet wouldn't move! Yet just like with the Rosenthal effect, which I told you about in chapter 1, circumstances shaped other people's perceptions, which in turn shaped reality. My new peers, who knew I was friends with Blake and frequented the Commons, already assumed I was a tough guy and interpreted my deer-in-headlights stance accordingly. Through their eyes, I was bravely standing my ground.

My mom and dad continued to fret about my appalling academic record, but to my lasting gratitude, my mom never once grounded me for bad grades, even as she didn't let me slide. She made it clear how disappointed she was with my school performance, and also insisted that I attend summer school. Keeping my social life out of bounds was one of those out-of-the-box decisions, but she knew how important it was for me to finally make friends, and was clearly enjoying watching me succeed. In this way, she contributed to a positive feedback loop that would have impacts reaching far into my future.

By that point, my mom was feeling more confident about a lot of her decisions. My dad's move up in life had inspired her, and her kids were at last becoming independent enough to give her more free time, so she resolved at last to pursue her old dream of becoming a nurse, following her spouse to Weber State.

As she spent less time at home, she had to rely on me and her other older kids more than before, and I relished that she was treating me as if I really was becoming more mature. We also occasionally even enjoyed each other's company.

Early one morning, near the end of my junior year at Layton High, I drove with my mom to sign up for a summer class she needed. While we were waiting in the line, which stretched clear into the parking lot, we watched a gorgeous blond college student drive up in a red Mazda Miata. My mom caught me drooling, and laughed, "Yeah, right, Todd. You're in high school, remember?"

I accepted the challenge, hopping out of the car but looking back to tell her, "Just watch." Within just an hour, I'd not only made a date, but had also convinced my new friend to let me drive her car. I slowed down as we passed my mother, still standing in line, to make sure to catch the look on her face when she recognized me.

I spent the rest of that day with the girl in the red Miata, and we went out on several more dates in the weeks thereafter. She came from an extremely wealthy family and must have assumed I did, too. She never realized I didn't have a car of my own, because after that first spin in her Miata, we always double-dated with a friend of mine who would drive. One evening, however, she said she wanted to park at my house and have me drive for a change.

I didn't know what to do. There was no way I was going to take this girl out in my mom's beat-up Chevy Cavalier, and my dad was adamant about not lending me his brand-new Toyota truck. My parents gave me that old *If she doesn't like you because you drive an old car, she isn't worth dating* blah blah blah. But then, as she pulled into our driveway, my mom happened to look out the window and saw she was driving her grandfather's car.

"Oh no, Todd, she's driving a Mercedes!" my mom blurted out. "A Mercedes!"

I pleaded with my dad one last time, but he refused to respond, instead silently turning away from me to head up the stairs. My mom answered the door and made some small talk with the girl, but then excused herself, saying she had to talk to me in private.

I followed her upstairs, where I heard my dad running the sink in their bathroom. My mom got out her purse and was starting to hand me twenty dollars, saying, "I'm sorry about the truck," but suddenly seemed to change her mind. Grabbing my dad's keys from the nightstand, she tossed them to me, shouting, "Run, Todd!" and then holding the bathroom door closed with all her might.

I rushed downstairs, hurried my date into the truck, and bolted out of the garage before my dad could get downstairs. We had a terrific time, and I got the truck back without a scratch, after which he nevertheless gave me (and my mom) the silent treatment for nearly a week.

By this time, my father had gotten used to his wife's thwarting his attempts to control me. If that hadn't been the case, I would doubtless have been sent off to military school well before then. Even so, Lyda was taking some risks with her marriage for the sake of my fledgling self-esteem. She more than anyone knew just how much I'd been hurting for so many years, and how giddy I was over my new social success.

Sure, dating a college girl isn't quite like hitting a game-winning shot for the varsity basketball team, or giving the valedictorian speech. At the time, however, it was the one activity that made me feel good about myself. So it meant everything to me that my mom would risk even my father's wrath to help me shine.

The Driver's Seat

My parents were both doing anything they could think of to get me to take school more seriously and improve my grades. They pleaded, nagged, threatened, and attempted bribes. At one point, my dad even offered to buy me a Porsche if I got all A's, likely because he assumed it would take a miracle for me even to get close. They were wasting their time and energy, however. Sure, bribes might have gotten me to go along with a few short-term objectives, like taking out the trash or finishing a homework assignment or two. But there was no way that money or promise of a fancy sports car was going to change my behavior in any serious or lasting way. It's not that I was lazy or stupid, or even uninterested in money. The reason I didn't care about my parents' objective for me is that I was already motivated, just by a different goal. The lure of social acceptance, at last, was far more potent than anything my parents had to offer.

Once again, modern neuroscience findings support my tales of woe. Researchers have shown that all behavior is goal-directed in one way or another. Brains simply don't function without goals. This may not seem like earth-shattering news, but just think how often you've heard a so-called expert—whether in education or psychology—talk about how some children are just not as "goal-directed" as other children. It's nonsense that gets in the way of many efforts to influence behavior for the better.

Plenty of recent research has made clear that people get significantly more engaged and motivated about doing things when they're pursuing goals that are authentic to them, rather than externally imposed. As the bestselling author Daniel Pink has pointed out in his excellent book, *Drive,* using carrots and sticks to shape behavior can therefore in fact be counterproductive, encouraging short-term thinking and even cheating, and snuffing out creativity. People's yearning for autonomy and mastery will beat carrots and sticks every time.

That's why parents and teachers who strategically work to first recognize what kids are trying to accomplish, and then help them achieve their initial, genuine goals, will get the best results down the line.

My younger son, Nathan, gave me a brilliant illustration of this rule a few years ago when he was in fifth grade. At this writing, Nathan is starting his sophomore year in high school, and is an excellent student. Back in elementary school, however, he'd acquired a reputation as a sweet kid who wasn't always as motivated as he should have been. Just before the holidays, his teacher sent me a greeting card with a picture of him in class and a note that said, "See what I mean?"

I looked at the photograph. Nathan looked absolutely joyful. He was sitting in front of a gingerbread structure he'd just made, with a huge smile on his face, and his arms in the air in a gesture of triumph. When I next saw his teacher and asked what was going on, she told me, with a sigh, that she'd assigned the class to make gingerbread houses, and doled out candy to decorate them. When Nathan, who has always had a sweet tooth, asked how much candy they could use, the teacher replied that they were free to take home as much as could fit on their houses.

This was when Nathan's drive kicked in. He realized that by building a gingerbread *fort*, he could take home the maximum amount of candy. By careful trial and error, he figured out a way to reinforce the walls with licorice so that they could bear the maximum amount of weight. The reason Nathan was so pleased with himself in the picture was that it had taken him ten minutes just to get the walls of the fort to stay up. The end result wasn't pretty, but it was beautifully functional. And he was proud.

Taking Care of Scooter

Once a kid starts to build up his self-esteem, as I was slowly doing at Layton High, it can lead to a lot of collateral progress. In my case, my new social standing gave me the self-assurance, for the first time in my life, to start showing more empathy toward other kids. I'm making a careful distinction here, between feeling and showing empathy, which "experts" on kids like I was seem to miss. I was always able to feel empathy. I knew quite well when other kids were hurting or struggling, as I was. I had simply rarely before felt moved (or sufficiently safe) to behave in an empathetic way. I'd experienced some of the worst of human nature in the way other kids had bullied me, and as far as I was concerned, anyone I noticed suffering had probably done something to deserve it.

But this, at least as I was now able to recognize, was not the case with Scooter. Scooter was a sophomore at Layton High, with fairly nondescript looks, and just a bit shorter than the rest of the kids his age. You might not remember him if you'd met him only once. He wasn't athletic, but he so eagerly wanted to belong that he volunteered to be the equipment manager for the football team. Scooter's dream was a seat in the Commons, and in pursuit of that ambition he used to ask me out to lunch and always volunteer to pay, because he knew I was usually short of cash. Sometimes, when I was really hungry, I'd let him.

One afternoon when I hadn't brought lunch money and was hankering for nachos, I suggested that Scooter take me to Taco Bell.

He turned pale at the mere mention of it. "There's no way we can go there," he muttered.

Apparently, some punk skateboarders had been tormenting Scooter's brother, who'd dated one of their girlfriends, and Scooter had been drawn into the fray as well. The punks had beaten them both up a couple of times, and also kicked the brother's car door in. Taco Bell was their hangout, and they'd warned Scooter that they'd send him to the hospital if he ever set foot there.

This situation cut way too close to home for me.

"We are going to Taco Bell, and I'm going to make sure nobody messes with you," I told Scooter.

When we arrived, the punks were already there. They glared at us throughout our meal, and when they left, the ringleader walked past us and muttered to Scooter, "Your babysitter isn't always going to be around." I didn't have the presence of mind to respond at the moment, and Scooter just stared at the ground. But later that day, as I sat in the Commons with my friends, I spotted the bully and his pals walking nearby. Without thinking much about it, I grabbed two stocky pals and headed in their direction, yelling the ringleader's name, with a few profanities for good measure. He stopped in front of the principal's office, while a crowd of rubbernecking students converged around us.

I pointed my finger in his face and said, "If you so much as look at Scooter again I am going to kick your ass. Do you understand me?"

"Screw you," he replied.

At that point, I carefully considered my options, and—okay, not really. I just punched him in the face.

I'd hit people before, but never like this. The head punk flew backward into the Plexiglas window of the principal's office, landing on the ground. Bloody and crying, he got to his feet and ran off. The principal yelled for me to come into his office, and once there, informed me he couldn't condone my behavior, and that I'd have to be punished for starting a fight. He suspended me for a day, yet at the end of his speech, caught my eye and gave me a silent thumbs-up. I felt like the punishment was worth it. I knew my dad wasn't going to be upset, because he'd always told me to stand up to bullies. Plus, from that day on, Scooter and his brother felt safe at school and went to Taco Bell whenever they felt like it.

All Downhill from Here

My social triumphs as an upperclassman continued to accumulate, offering a dramatic contrast to the generally depressing slide of the rest of my life.

Not only was I failing most of my classes, I was still doing a lot of rash and crazy things that only by great good luck never got me thrown into juvenile hall. I was a senior, for example, when I briefly got involved in the scheme to sell fake IDs, which neither my parents, nor, luckily, the police, ever discovered.

What can I say today, nearly twenty years later? These memories are embarrassing to me, and yet adolescents tend to do stupid things, and adolescent boys with poor self-control, unsurprisingly, do the stupidest things of all. Once again my parents were unaware of most of what was going on, but they knew about the bad grades, and we argued every night about my lack of motivation and poor work ethic. The arguing never really bothered me, but I'll never forget the sight of my father, shortly after he opened what I later understood would be my final report card from Layton High. This time he didn't yell—he just sat down on the staircase and sobbed. I'd never seen him cry before, and the sight of it shook me with the realization that I wasn't the only person affected by my choices. Yet even then, I didn't start trying to turn things around for the simple reason that I honestly didn't believe I could.

Whenever I actually showed up in class, all through high school, my teachers would pester me. They'd been telling me the same thing for years now—that it was clear I was smart, so why wasn't I trying harder? Yet that tactic, as I've since learned, was almost guaranteed to backfire. Telling kids they're smart but just need to "try harder" rarely if ever gets them to do that. In fact, it often creates a perverse incentive not to try. The child may well have already stopped trying because he has lost faith that he can succeed. So from where he sits, it is better to have someone think he's smart and is choosing not to try rather than trying and certainly failing. If he tries and fails, he'll have lost even that slim promise.

Stanford psychologist Carol Dweck, when she was based at Columbia University, published pioneering research that underlies this point. In a study of four hundred fifth-graders, the children took two tests, the second of which was made so hard that every child failed. By the third test, children who had been praised for their effort bounced back sufficiently to achieve scores that were 30 percent higher than on the first test. But students who were praised for their smarts had scores that were 20 percent lower. The researchers concluded that parents and teachers can be most effective when they praise kids for abilities, like effort, that are under their control.

As I look back today on my own stubborn stance in high school, it still strikes me as reasonable. Given what I have since found out about learning, and particularly how much it depends on a good "fit" with one's environment, I honestly don't believe I could have been successful had I tried harder. The sad truth is that my school could not have supported and challenged me in the way that I needed. So, as is the case with many other struggling students, I was essentially set up to fail. My only available choice was to go down fighting, so that's what I did.

To my mother's added anguish, my rebellion extended to our family's faith. It was generally assumed, among good Mormon families, that at age nineteen, every young man would head out for a two-year "mission" to spread the gospel anywhere in the world that the church elders chose to send you. But by the time we moved to Layton, it was clear to everyone who knew me that a mission didn't figure in my plans. To their credit, my mom and dad never pressured me to change my mind, even as they bore the brunt of their neighbors' judgment about this further sign of my presumably bad character.

All this helps explain that when I first started going out with Kaylin, the young woman who in less than a year would be my wife, her devout Mormon parents weren't exactly fainting with joy.

We met in twelfth grade, about a year after I enrolled at Layton High. We sat near each other in seminary class (the Mormon equivalent of Bible study), held in a brick building across from the campus, and I couldn't stop staring at her. She was blond and petite, with porcelain skin, and while she never would have been kicked out of the Commons, I could see she was also quite shy. I suspected she might not be good at small talk, so I decided to give us a reason to communicate. When she left her desk to go to the restroom, I stole her Bible and put it on my desk. This was the kind of ploy that would have been viewed as purely annoying in my old high school, but by then the world was seeing me in an entirely different light. When Kaylin returned and saw me with the book, she looked puzzled, but not angry. So I took the initiative and made her a deal: the book for her phone number. We had our first date the same week.

Kaylin and I were inseparable from that point on, but she paid a high price for the romance. Shortly after our first date, her friend Amy, a straight-laced girl from an upstanding Mormon family, was banned by her parents from seeing Kaylin anymore, on the grounds that I was such an obvious loser, with no plans for college, a career, or even a Mormon mission. What's more, I'm sure Kaylin's religiously devout dad also felt justified in his own poor opinion of me after he discovered that I'd convinced his daughter to use his credit card to pay for about $1,200 in food and gasoline for my friends.

Worse ignominy was to come, however. About two-thirds of the way through my senior year, my parents called me in to our dining room for a talk. They'd visited the principal, who'd told them that at that point, there was no way I was going to have enough credits to graduate. I had a 0.09 grade point average for that semester, and a 1.5 cumulative average for my junior and senior years. My mom said the principal had "suggested" that they take me out of school and have me take the General Educational Development test (GED) for an equivalent of a high school diploma. Then he told them that I would no longer be allowed on the high school campus.

The news was not a huge surprise. I'd known I was in danger

of failing, and had even signed up for summer school the previous year, although my discipline failed me after just a couple weeks and I stopped showing up for class. My parents had then pushed me to sign up for night school that year to make up the credits, only to find, once again, that I was pretending to attend, but instead just enjoying the free nights out with friends.

As they sat with me around the dining room table, my mom kept saying how worried she was about what would become of me, but my dad just said he was fed up. "From here on in, if you want to keep on living with us, you're going to have to start contributing," he announced. "It's time for you to get a job."

Now that I was eighteen, he said, he wasn't willing to let me lounge around doing nothing and going nowhere on his dime. Had my mom been the one to say this, I probably wouldn't have taken it seriously, but my dad, in my experience, never said anything he didn't mean, and when he showed me the budget he had drawn up, detailing what it would cost me to rent an apartment on my own, I realized I had better take his advice.

"You Don't Have to Marry Him"

Within a week after that pivotal talk with my parents, I found myself a job stocking shelves in a department store for $4.25 an hour, then the minimum wage in Utah. It was one of the few jobs listed in the classified ad section that didn't require a high school diploma. I don't remember feeling especially sad as I resigned myself to this daily monotony. At that point, I still had no real reason to think much about the future. My circle of friends was still my first priority, and I didn't think leaving high school would mean I'd stop seeing them. On the other hand, from my first day on the job, I was bored out of my mind. This, I discovered, was much worse than sitting in class day after day. But there was no going back, it seemed—and especially not after Kaylin suddenly told me her own world-changing news. Eight months into our courtship, she was pregnant.

Kaylin's father by then disliked me so much that he declared himself willing even to tolerate a child born out of wedlock if it meant avoiding linking our lives together. "You don't have to marry him," he told her repeatedly, often even when I was standing right there. But Kaylin was in love and also more than ready to leave home. To prepare for my new life as a responsible married man, I switched to a slightly higher-paying but even more boring job, as an aluminum factory assembly-line worker: punching a clock, wearing a cotton jumpsuit uniform, and filling shifts alongside a woman with a mustache. I lasted there just one week.

We got married just before Kaylin started to need to wear maternity clothes, in the small basketball court of our Mormon church, which community members could use for free. Kaylin's father, as a wedding present, absolved me of the $1,200 debt from the charges on his credit card.

Kaylin's mother sewed her dress for her, while one of her sisters baked our cake. Her brother served as amateur photographer—so amateur that every picture in our album has a curious pink ring around the outside. Only immediate family and a few friends attended, and my family discouraged any potential extravagances, such as bouquets or formal invitations, for fear of sending the wrong message to my younger siblings.

"Now you will obey your husband as you obeyed me," Kaylin's father intoned, as he stood at the altar. I caught my dad's eye, and he shrugged, and we exchanged a smile. That whole obedient-wife concept was not exactly dogma in our own house.

For our honeymoon, Kaylin and I drove to Nevada with my grandparents, who generously subsidized the trip. We stayed for two nights in a $29-per-night motel in Wendover, about two hours from Salt Lake City, and a common destination for Mormons sneaking over the border to gamble. Mostly we played board games in our room, but a couple times I went with my grandmother to the casinos, even though, at nineteen, I was two years shy of the legal gambling age.

I had yet to reach my twentieth birthday six months later, when, back in Utah, in a dimly lit hospital room, I held my newborn son, Austin, in my arms, and wept. It was July 11, 1994— the day it hit me that, for the first time in my life, other people were depending on me, and that somehow or other I was going to have to live up to their trust.

BIG IDEAS
• ▪ • ▪ • ▪ • ▪ • ▪

- If you offer your child a Porsche as a bribe if he gets straight A's, make sure to clearly state that the deal expires in high school, lest your child go on to get straight A's throughout all of college and graduate school and then expect you to keep your promise. (Mom? Dad?)

- Goals matter. Every behavior is goal-directed for the simple reason that brains simply don't function without goals. It makes no sense to assume that a child is not goal-directed, when the problem is more that we don't understand the goal that is motivating his or her behavior.

- The powerful role of emotions ensures that having friends—or at least, preventing complete social isolation— will almost always trump academic achievement for a child.

- Sometimes a fresh start can be a miracle cure for a struggling child—a way to reboot the context. Yet for that second chance to be useful, the child needs to understand *why* things didn't work in the old context, and have a sense for what he or she can do to avoid repeating past mistakes.

- Feeling empathy and showing it are two different things. If a child is constantly picked on and bullied, he may be capable of the former but not the latter.

ACTION ITEMS
• ▪ • ▪ • ▪ • ▪ • ▪ • ▪

▪ Remember how I learned social skills from mimicking Jimmy, and make sure that as you model your very best behavior for your kids, you also support their spending time with other kids who are smart about relationships.

▪ If you want to change your child's behavior, start by trying to understand the goals that are motivating it.

▪ Find an opportunity to admit a genuine mistake to your child. Tell him or her not only what you did, but also what you learned from it.

▪ When praising your child, remember that you can be most effective when you focus on factors, such as effort, that are within his control.

▪ Before you ask your child to "try harder," evaluate whether that's really the problem.

· 6 ·

Social Justice

"The first rule is that you must not fool yourself, and you are the easiest person to fool."

—RICHARD FEYNMAN

The Microphone Test

A few years ago, in the name of scientific inquiry, I decided to really stress out my students. I was about five weeks into a course I teach at Harvard called Educational Neuroscience, and had led my class of roughly one hundred graduate students through the basics of brain architecture, perception, and memory. We had just moved on to consider recent research about the role of emotions in learning, when out of the blue, I told the students I was going to pick one of them at random to give the rest of the group a brief lecture on the role of neuroscience in education. The task itself would be simple: The person I chose would merely have to summarize what we'd learned to date. No big deal, right?

"You can now have two minutes to take some notes on what you might say, but you can't take your notes with you to the podium," I explained.

I projected a slide onto the screen in the front of the room, showing the scene the lucky student I picked would have to face: a close-up photograph of an enormous microphone, in front of a sea of expectant faces. I took out my pocket timer to count down the two minutes.

The impact was immediate, obvious, and also quite startling, especially considering that so many of these students were planning to make a career of standing up in front of a group, five days a week, to teach. Some students gasped. One woman actually sprang from her desk and escaped through a back door. As my timer ticked down to zero, I could tell that quite a few of the people in the room were literally panicking. Their minds went blank, as they later described it. Several said they felt incapable of taking a single note. (Remember what I told you in chapter 4 about how stress plays havoc with your working memory.)

"Ten seconds," I warned, theatrically pacing in front of my lectern. Then, "Time's up! The lucky winner is—"

I looked around the room, drawing out the suspense, and then said, "Okay. So just kidding. I'm not going to actually have you give the talk."

I heard a few more gasps, now mixed with laughter and sighs of relief.

"But I do want to talk about the experience," I added.

I asked first for comments from people who had felt just fine about the test. A student sitting up in front immediately began waving his hand.

"Things have just been clicking for me in this class," he said. As he went on to explain, he'd begun to feel the course was especially relevant to his life, after he had recently suffered an illness that his doctor attributed to stress. He was excited by this new, visceral understanding of the connection between his emotions and mental and physical health.

I then called on another student, who, with similar confidence, said, "I'm a teacher. I thought I'll just take some notes and see what comes out." Having already survived similar tests, in other words, she knew she could get through this one.

Gramling's Anthem

After hearing from a couple more of these buoyant folk, I asked for a show of hands of people who'd had a negative reaction. The first to respond was Maleka Donaldson Gramling, normally one of my most enthusiastic students, and someone I'd pegged as an extrovert, not least because she'd been a member of a Harvard choir as an undergraduate and had gone on to sing in a world fusion band. On tour with the choir, she had once performed in front of ten thousand people at an outdoor concert in Germany.

Still, Gramling had frozen up in the face of the microphone test. She confessed that she hadn't been able to take a single note, holding up her blank page to prove it.

"I was surprised at myself," she said quietly. She'd never had any trouble recalling what she'd learned in class while relating it to family and friends afterward. Moreover, Gramling added: "I don't get nervous when I'm *singing.*" Yet when I suggested that she give the mini-lecture, she said, "Everything just left my brain, and it was like, no, I just talked about this! But what am I going to say? And then I hear you go: 'Ten seconds!'"

As so often—even now—still happens, I didn't stop to think about the possible consequences of what I said next. "You wanna come sing?" I asked her.

"You serious? Okay!"

Without any further hesitation, she walked up in front of the picture of the mike, placed her hands on her hips, closed her eyes, and belted out a spine-tinglingly beautiful rendition of "The Star-Spangled Banner." The rest of the class cheered her soaring high notes. She smiled and returned to her seat.

I shook my head in wonder. My experiment could easily have gone either way, of course. Gramling might have bombed, and been permanently scarred by that experience in my classroom, in which case her fellow students likely would have judged me as a sadist. Instead, there she was, just a minute after having freaked out about not being able to speak to a class of her peers, singing to us as if she were at Fenway Park. It was obvious to me and the other students alike that at that moment she saw herself as a completely different person from the one who had panicked just a few minutes before. And this simple change in perspective had a real-time effect on her ability to perform.

When I look back on Gramling's anthem today, I consider it the turning point in my own perspective: the moment I was genuinely sold on the enormous relevance of emotions in both learning and behavior. To be sure, I'd already been aware of a great deal of intriguing new research on the power of emotions, which I was including in my lectures. Yet together with many of my colleagues, I still wasn't entirely convinced of the strength of the connection—until I saw it so plainly demonstrated.

Emotions Rule

I owe the idea for the microphone test to my colleague Gabrielle Rappolt-Schlichtmann. For several weeks leading up to that day in class, she'd been trying to convince me about how new findings on emotions and cognition (rational thought) show that when we're dealing with the brain, emotions must no longer be seen as the proverbial icing on the cake—they're really much more like the batter.

This notion, championed so far most famously by the neuroscientist and bestselling author Antonio Damasio, is gaining adherents as evidence accumulates that brain areas linked to emotion are much more crucial than we'd ever thought in governing behavior. As Damasio and his colleagues have shown, people with damage to these brain areas tend to make seemingly irrational and often self-destructive decisions, and lose their ability to learn from their mistakes, even if their "rational" brain networks remain intact. While this may at first seem unlikely, it starts to make more sense when you recall that we humans evolved as social animals, and that reading emotional signals has long been far more critical to our survival than reading words on a page.

Rappolt-Schlictmann's own pioneering research bears this out. She has focused primarily on studying ways in which preschool teachers can help unusually stressed children calm down enough to make learning possible. In studies of preschoolers from low-income, high-stress families, she and her team have monitored the children's levels of cortisol—the stress hormone I told you about in chapter 4. She found that these levels drop significantly—on average about 10 percent—when the kids are placed in smaller groups, with teachers trained to speak softly and help them feel secure. (Note to parents: feel free to try this at home.)

Many kids in poverty are chronically stressed, since they come from environments in which they often need to be especially vigilant to keep themselves safe and fed. If they then are placed in a chaotic classroom, they'll likely feel threatened instead of challenged. At that point, learning becomes a low priority, and in fact all but impossible, as the child devotes all of his or her energy to the limited choice of fight or flight.

It's worth keeping in mind that stress is not always a negative factor. Indeed, some stress is needed to keep us awake and alert. The tricky thing to figure out is when that healthy sense of *challenge* increases to a harmful sense of *threat*, because that tipping point varies from person to person, even though the physiological consequences do not.

Stress Is Subjective

The dramatic variability in the way people experience stressful events helps explain the diversity of responses by my students to the microphone test. For some, the pressure was a net plus: They felt motivated by watching me pace back and forth with my timer. Yet approximately one in four of them "choked" under that same pressure. What made the difference had nothing to do with intelligence—some of the top-performing students went blank, swamped by the physiological response to stress—but rather with a combination of factors, having to do with both their innate biology and all of their experience to date.

This is just one example of the principle I introduced in chapter 4—that there is no such thing as an *objective* threat. The sensation of being threatened is an emotional and subjective reaction. For some students, such as those who've had several bad experiences in the classroom, the mere possibility of a teacher calling on them at random may raise their blood levels of stress hormones by just as much as if they had heard a lion roar from within their bedroom closet.

As scientists offer increasingly powerful evidence about how debilitating excessive and prolonged stress can be for students, both in terms of their learning potential and their mental health, teachers and parents will have to rethink some of the rules that have governed classrooms for so long. After the microphone test, for instance, one of my students, who'd been teaching for several years, said he would no longer call on students without warning. Looking more closely, however, how can we get better at spotting that critical threshold at which healthy stress rises to the point of a threat? For each student, this will depend on a unique balance of *demands and resources*.

This model of evaluating behavior under pressure was first articulated in 1996 by psychologists Jim Blascovich and Joe Tomaka, who reviewed scores of research studies involving people obliged to perform various tasks—from taking a test, to giving a speech, to trying to sell someone something. They concluded that individuals generally feel challenged to a healthy degree when they evaluate—often unconsciously—that their resources are at least roughly equal to the demands of a given situation.

If demands exceed a person's resources, however, he or she is likely to feel threatened.

Now, both demands and resources can include concrete *and* highly subjective factors. The demands involved in a given task will include not only the level of sheer effort required but also an individual's perceptions of the danger and uncertainty involved. Resources can include anything from skills, equipment, knowledge, familiarity, and experience to whether a person slept well the previous night. Resources can also include a person's disposition: On the afternoon of the microphone test, one particularly sanguine student in my class asked, "What do I care if I stand up and make a fool out of myself?"

Blascovich and Tomaka and the many researchers who followed them have carefully described the contrasting physiologies of perceived challenge versus threat. Both emotional states involve a slightly accelerated heart rate, as if a person were engaged in mild aerobic exercise. Yet when someone is threatened, as opposed to challenged, his or her arteries will constrict, increasing blood pressure. This is the physiological state best suited for running away from a predator, but not for performing well on cognitive tasks; the limbs are energized at the expense of the brain. In the worst-case scenario, the perception of threat leads to the classic fight-or-flight response, where panic overrides rationality. It can be triggered by a real-life danger (like that lion), or even by memories—like a student who has been humiliated once before—that lead to the *anticipation* of danger. For your average grade-school child, a few brushes with a bully combined with some charged encounters with a principal or teacher can make school feel like such a hostile place that simply *thinking* about it can trigger a threat response. And remember, even though you—as the parent or teacher—might "know" that the student is not in any danger, it doesn't matter. It literally doesn't matter. If the student perceives threat, the consequences are the same. The child walks into the classroom prepared, at best, to survive, but not to learn.

The implications of all this for parents, teachers, and students, are huge. To help kids do their best in school, we have to get smarter about analyzing the challenge-versus-threat dynamic and how it breaks down in such a varied way for each individual. The good news is that there are many efforts in progress to do just that.

One promising field of study involves examining the enormous degree to which perceptions of social support—or lack thereof—can influence this balance of demands and resources. Do a student's teachers or classmates believe he'll do well? If you remember the Rosenthal effect (from chapter 1), it won't surprise you that this will have a lot to do with whether he actually will. The phenomenon has been particularly elegantly illustrated by an experiment at San Francisco's Exploratorium, one of the best science museums in this country. Visitors stand in a booth where they are instructed to speak into a microphone, while a sound track plays applause. It's enough to make anyone more confident.

Interestingly enough, researchers have recently discovered that even as simple an intervention as having students write a brief essay about their worries before taking a test can significantly boost their scores. This sort of technique has proven to be especially helpful with members of minorities, women, and particularly anxious students. One project found that asking African-American students to reaffirm their values throughout the school year can reduce the normal race-related achievement gap by the end of the year. These are all compelling illustrations of how what we think we know isn't static, or simply dependent on how much we've studied, but changes according to circumstances.

Context can also have a powerfully negative influence on learning, however, which is how it more often works with kids like me. In particular, there's a dynamic known as *stereotype threat*, first described in the mid-1990s by the social psychologist Claude Steele, which refers to the way someone can internalize what he or she feels are other people's negative expectations and proceed to fulfill that prophecy. In other words, if someone tells you before you take a math test that people like you— troublemakers, kids diagnosed with ADHD, but also frazzled moms, women, African-Americans, senior citizens, or other specifically defined groups—don't usually do well on math tests, you will likely perform more poorly than if he or she hadn't said it.

The "stereotype threat" research provides one of the most clear-cut examples of how emotions are intimately woven together with thinking and learning. It also lays bare how amazingly important it is to never lose sight of the fact that behavior and learning are the results of complex systems—always dependent on the unique way in which each child interacts with his environment.

As people become more aware of the tremendous variability in how people learn, on top of other types of diversity such as race, culture, and income, schools are gradually paying more attention to the danger of negative expectations. So far, however, considerably more attention has been focused on a more immediate and tangible campus threat: the surprisingly widespread problem of bullying.

Bullying Bans and Other Emotional Support

As I mentioned in chapter 4, there has been a notable recent increase in public concern about bullying: the most obvious way that students are emotionally sabotaged at school. Many school administrators have jumped on the antibullying bandwagon, instituting a wide range of educational and disciplinary tactics. Some of these are promising, but many others have been well-intentioned flops. While at this writing, there's relatively little research on the most effective programs, the work that has been done suggests schools have considerable power to prevent children from being systematically intimidated, and given all we know about the effects of the threat response on learning, it behooves us to step up to the challenge. Some recent studies suggest that the most successful programs have decreased bullying by up to 23 percent.

At this writing, the strategy that has won the most kudos is the Olweus Bullying Prevention Program, a multicomponent, school-wide model first implemented in Norway in 1970 by the Swedish research psychologist Dan Olweus, and since copied in schools in the United States and elsewhere throughout the world. Among its most effective tools are outreach to families, including parent-education sessions, teacher training, and attentive supervision during recess hours.

Unfortunately, some antibullying programs end up doing more harm than good. Typically these failures will hand off too much power to the kids involved, such as with so-called peer-mentoring or peer-led conflict resolution. Cambridge University criminologists David Farrington and Maria Ttofi have published the most comprehensive studies to date examining antibullying programs and have found that grouping kids together in attempts to combat bullying and other oppositional behavior often makes the bad behavior more widespread through contagion.

Other researchers have criticized programs focused on conflict resolution, even when adults are in charge, since when a bully is involved, such efforts mistakenly frame the problem as between two peers of equal power, rather than between a more powerful student who is mistreating someone who is weaker.

Simply jawboning about bad behavior at school—be it bullying or a range of other offenses—tends to do little good, researchers have found, with the "Just Say No" so-called drug prevention programs being a leading example. And least useful of all, in general, and often downright counterproductive, are the zero-tolerance policies now common at many schools, which automatically suspend children who break rules having to do with bullying or other forbidden behaviors. These draconian policies have yet to prove their effectiveness and may actually tend to reduce reporting of bullying, since victims and witnesses may be reluctant to take responsibility for ending the school career of a young person who may be just as emotionally troubled as his victim.

It's not exactly rocket science to figure out that being chronically teased or bullied, or socially isolated, can kill a student's interest in school. Beyond targeting bullying, many schools are wisely trying to help improve students' lives with a flood of new programs that emphasize social and emotional skills. In 2011, the first major analysis of these programs showed that in general they have not only helped many children improve their relationships, but they have also had a significant impact on academic achievement. The study, which appeared in the January/February 2011 issue of the journal *Child Development*, was conducted by scientists at two universities based in Chicago, and looked at more than two hundred school-based social and emotional learning programs, involving approximately 270,000 K–12 students. The programs included classroom instruction by teachers and visiting experts, mostly focused on managing emotions and relationships and setting and achieving smart goals. When managed well, these programs can significantly help adjust that key balance of demands and resources for kids. Researchers have discovered several benefits, including a decline in students' misbehavior and anxiety, and, most surprisingly, an average 11 percent gain in performance on achievement tests.

To be sure, the efforts aren't always graceful. For some schools, "social-emotional learning" has become a catchphrase for overindulging in political correctness. Some schools have gone so far as to eliminate competitive sports so that no child has to experience the pain of losing—a move I think is misdirected, at best. (There is nothing wrong with learning to compete fairly, and there is a lot to gain by learning to "lose well.") Others, however, have carefully built school cultures that shore up students' emotional resources with understanding and respect.

High School Havens

The best example I've encountered to date of a school culture that provides this key support can be found at High Tech High, which is in fact a group of (at last count) eleven charter schools in Southern California. The schools are so popular that admissions are determined by an annual lottery. At last count, there were ten applications for every student enrolled.

Founded in 2000, the network at this writing includes two elementary schools, four middle schools, and five high schools. Its main campus, a former U.S. Navy engineering training center near the San Diego airport, is a light and airy showcase of the modernity that inspires both its tactics and curriculum. Students have ample room to stretch out, mentally and physically, with thirty-nine thousand square feet for four hundred teenagers. Beneath high ceilings with exposed steel beams, classrooms are set off with fifteen-foot glass walls. Visitors walk through halls lined with prize-winning science projects—a set of bicycle wheels that illustrates physics principles; there, a wall-hanging demonstrating the mechanics of how music is made, by showing the inside of a piano.

The school's original backers were local business leaders who shared dismay over the failure of public education to guarantee a well-prepared workforce. Early on, they attracted the pivotal support of the Bill & Melinda Gates Foundation. They also recruited education reformer Larry Rosenstock, who became its founding principal, CEO, chief advocate, and charismatic guru.

Rosenstock is a lean, balding man who talks like he's trying to catch a bus and even then seems to have trouble keeping up with his own thoughts. Nearly every inch of wall space in his large office is filled with posters and photographs and students' work, including portraits of Albert Einstein (whom Rosenstock refers to as "Albie"), Mao, Muhammad Ali, and a chimpanzee. A warning sign says: "No Snivelling."

Before Rosenstock moved to San Diego, he lectured at Harvard's Graduate School of Education, taught high school carpentry, and directed the New Urban High School Project, funded by the U.S. Department of Education. In his first year at High Tech High, he told an interviewer that his main goal was to change the relationship between teachers and students, "with teachers becoming more like guides and mentors and students more like active learners who can develop their interests and passions and pursue them." By all appearances, he has done just that.

When you walk through the halls at High Tech High schools, you see teenagers who look startlingly unlike those you might encounter at most other high schools in this country. They are, for the most part, truly animated, smiling and chatting. The charter school status has given Rosenstock extraordinary power to challenge top-down traditions that leave so many U.S. students alienated at best and victimized at worst. Hands-on, collaborative work is the norm rather than the exception. Teachers are paid at above-average rates for California, but aren't eligible for tenure, and as part of the hiring process must audition in front of real classes, after which students are asked for their impressions.

"A lot of our secret is made up of what we *don't* do," says Rosenstock. There is no public-address system, nor bells to signal the start and end of class. Teachers and students use the same bathrooms. And there's none of the danger of anonymity that pervades so many high schools. A basic rule is that every student knows there is at least one adult on campus who feels personally responsible for his or her success and well-being. Beyond their time in the classroom, teachers are expected to make meaningful connections with students and their families, visiting each of their homes once a year, and serving as advisors to the same students throughout their four years in school.

These strategies have produced exceptional success, both in the schools' strong sense of community and the students' academic achievement. High Tech High's graduation rates are dramatically higher than other California schools, while Rosenstock says that a remarkable 70 percent of their students go on to four-year colleges. This is despite the fact that, as news of the school's success has spread, parents of kids who have struggled in traditional schools have flocked to apply, raising the rate of such students well beyond the local norm.

The schools are so unusually supportive of kids with all kinds of learning variability that High Tech High's contract psychologist, Mark Katz, once led a tour of the campus for fellow mental health professionals who'd been asking to learn more. He dubbed the field trip "Beyond the Pill," signaling his belief, which I strongly share, that a great deal of the psychotropic medications now in use today would become much less necessary if we adults could just learn to manage our kids' environments more intelligently.

One of the best things about High Tech High, to my mind, is that Rosenstock and other administrators don't waste time talking very much about "social-emotional" learning. Instead they simply provide a radically different learning context that nurtures all kinds of children. And when I say "nurture," I don't mean "coddle." Rather, it's a matter of making kids feel better understood, and more valued and supported, while allowing their strengths to emerge. No student is penalized for lacking skills that are all but impossible for some to master. As an example, support for note-taking is offered in all classes. As a rule, the teacher will assign and pay one particularly proficient student to take notes that will then be available to others who might need them.

Luckily for an increasing number of U.S. kids, High Tech High's focus on building more supportive environments isn't unique. More and more school directors, particularly at charter and private schools, are starting to see the light, and working to engineer more effective ways for students to get an education than to sit numbly, hour after hour, at their desks.

Of course, some schools have been rebelling against conventional education for many years. On the East Coast, the private Sudbury Valley School, founded in 1968 in Framingham, Massachusetts, retains that era's antiestablishment philosophy, updated with an emphasis on computer technology's power to liberate kids from their desks. The school, housed in an old stone mansion and converted barn on a mid-nineteenth-century estate, gives students exceptional autonomy in making decisions that affect them. It also maintains a policy of intermingling kids of all ages, from preschool to high school, a tactic that researchers who've studied the school say has encouraged older students to behave more responsibly, as nurturers and mentors. Maybe it didn't work out this well in *Lord of the Flies*, but researchers say the approach of schooling big kids with little kids has virtually eliminated bullying.

More generally, I'm convinced that this kind of careful consideration of context offers the most powerful check on all kinds of student misbehavior, as well as the best way to ensure that kids meet their potential at school. Ample research shows that when kids feel less powerless and bored and more positively connected to adults and peers at their school, they tend to excel, emotionally, socially, and academically. In an online column titled "School Bullying: A Tragic Cost of Forced Schooling and Autocratic School Governance," Boston College research psychologist Peter Gay compared the top-down power structure prevalent at most schools to prisons and the Chinese feudal system, theorizing that it's only natural to expect that students would rebel whenever they could get away with it, or even when they couldn't, just as happens in China and in prisons. Bullying occurs regularly in settings where people have no political power, as Gay notes, and, in most cases, as long as the guards and wardens—or teachers—have more interest in hiding the problem than confronting it effectively. In contrast, when students feel that they have genuine power over their environment, they have a vested interest in keeping it both peaceful and successful.

So, once again, the key is in the context. If you want young people to learn empathy, don't just talk about it. Place them in supportive, democratic, and fair-minded environments free of cruelty—for instance, where no teacher would consider punishing, much less ridiculing, a student with a lousy short-term memory—and where empathy flows naturally. Then just sit back and watch the miracles happen, like me sticking up for Scooter, or Maleka Gramling singing "The Star-Spangled Banner" to a hundred of her peers.

BIG IDEAS
• ▪ • ▪ • ▪ • ▪

- A student's ability to learn depends on his or her emotional state, which itself depends on context.

- Emotions usually have a far greater impact than "pure" rationality in determining whether we make good decisions.

- A little stress can help someone learn, while too much stress prevents it. The optimal amount of stress varies from person to person.

- Whether someone is challenged and engaged, or, conversely, threatened and shut down, depends on a balance of *demands* and *resources*. Demands include anything from the difficulty of the task at hand to the person's perception of other people's reactions. Resources include factors such as perceived skills, available materials and support, and individual temperament.

ACTION ITEMS
● ■ ● ■ ● ■ ● ■ ● ■ ● ■ ●

- Pay attention to how much stress your child is under, at home and at school, and whether your child is feeling threatened versus challenged.

- Particularly if you notice that most of your interactions with your admittedly challenging child have become negative, try a few "random acts of kindness" to see if you can't initiate a positive feedback loop.

- Some U.S. high schools have managed to create cultures that support learning by nurturing students' emotional resources. It's worth a parent's time to evaluate how your child's school measures up, and, if possible, find ways to support improvements.

Turnaround

"Good judgment comes from experience. Experience
comes from bad judgment."

—MULLA NASRUDIN

Minimum Wage Days

Because of how much time has passed, and how much better
our lives have become in recent years, my parents and Kaylin and
I can now laugh about all the ways I used to drive them nuts—
not least being how I worked at no fewer than ten jobs within the
two years after our first son was born.

From that day that I first held Austin in my arms, I'd been
telling everyone who would listen that becoming a father had
changed me to the core. I was finally ready to apply myself, I
declared, and to work hard to support my new family. Yet I still
couldn't manage to stick to any particular employment for longer
than three months at a time.

I went from stocking shelves in a department store to making
aluminum sheets on an assembly line to manning ovens for a
bagel franchise on the predawn shift, to working the phones in a

credit card customer service department, to selling chain-link fence, door-to-door, across northern Utah.

I never got fired from any of these jobs, and almost always at least initially won praise from my bosses for my high energy and productivity. Yet as soon as I learned the routine, I'd get so bored that I wouldn't be able to tolerate another day, and then I'd quit. This struck many people around me at the time (including, and most notably, my in-laws) as even worse than getting fired, since to them work was not ever supposed to be enjoyable, but more something that you endured. Kaylin's dad thought he understood the problem, pronouncing me "inherently lazy."

To no one's surprise, we were always short of money. Not long before Austin was born, Kaylin and I had moved out of my parents' basement and into a one-bedroom apartment about two miles away. It was our declaration of independence, the start of our life as genuine adults, but luxury wasn't its strong suit. The place measured barely 450 square feet—so small that I could lie on my stomach in the middle of the apartment and have a body part in every room: the kitchen, bathroom, front room, and a bedroom so tiny that it could barely contain both our bed and Austin's crib. The other little problem was that I couldn't afford even the first month's rent. To my huge embarrassment and relief, my mom quietly came to our rescue, writing the check on my promise that I had a plan to repay her.

She might have known better. Our financial situation was only getting worse, with my average pay so low that Kaylin and I depended on a generous friend to donate diapers. After a stack of bills piled up, we finally applied for welfare assistance, and stayed on welfare for the next three humiliating years. Kaylin supplemented our income by selling blood as often as once a week, which was as frequent as the law allows.

Sad to say, there were more than a few occasions after we'd start to save a little money that my impulsivity caught up with me, and I'd do something that would push us back to the far side of precarious. Barely one week after I'd been hired at a new, commissions-only sales job at an electronics store, for instance, I used my lunch break to wander over to a nearby car lot and, on a whim, bought a new blue Honda Civic I could in no way afford. The car would soon be repossessed, and that one dumb move would spoil our credit for several years to come.

In view of all this, it's easy for me to imagine how someone looking at my life from the outside might have concluded that I really hadn't changed. In many ways, I was still behaving like the goofy kid who'd thrown a rock at a car for no reason, and the slacker teen who'd skipped school to take his buddies to break-fast with his ill-gotten gains. Nonetheless, I have no doubt to-day that beneath that discouraging appearance, I was indeed changing—slowly, subtly, but also fundamentally.

The Man in the Mirror

If I had to set a date for the start of those changes that led to my transformation from junior hoodlum to Harvard applicant, it would be the day I stood up for Scooter back at Layton High. My unprecedented decision to act on an empathetic impulse and defend the bullies' victim was a major turning point for me: the moment I authentically signed up as part of a larger community.

Sure, I was getting at least somewhat more mature as I got older, but my transformation was more complicated than that. Until that time, and most likely due to so many years of being socially isolated, I had seriously doubted the goodness of human nature, not least my own. But my new circle of friends in high school had made me feel not only accepted but worthwhile, and, for the first time, I felt I truly owed other people my best efforts.

Getting married to Kaylin hugely added to my new feeling of self-worth, which in turn opened the door to other previously impossible changes. Slowly at first, but then more and more, I became more honest with myself. I still made many stupid mistakes, but for the first time that I could recall, I was able not only to acknowledge blunders after I made them, but also to try to figure out how they'd happened. In other words, I was increasingly able to learn from my mistakes.

Of course, many well-adjusted people acquire this skill in childhood, but people like me, for some good reasons, have a harder time. Part of the problem is that from a very early age, I'd made so many dumb mistakes that I'd gotten in the habit of denying or explaining them away, out of the fear that if I didn't, I'd be confirmed as an unredeemable screwup. I got so good at this that I even fooled myself. Blaming other people or circumstances for my own blunders was the way I managed to live with myself. In the early years of my marriage, however, I mustered the courage to drop some of those excuses and face myself more honestly. My new ability to recognize the good parts of myself helped me to address the parts that needed improvement.

Many years later, I came across some research that helps explain this process. It's part of a new niche of psychology, inspired by Buddhist philosophy, that has been establishing some dramatic benefits of "self-compassion," or, more plainly, being kind to oneself. Researchers have found that people who score relatively high on tests of self-compassion are less depressed and anxious, and more happy and optimistic than others.

University of Texas psychologist Kristin Neff, a pioneer in this field, takes pains to contrast self-compassion with self-indulgence, a point I agree is well worth making. Rather than being a way to spoil yourself, she suggests, genuine self-compassion can serve as a check on the kind of relentless self-criticism that keeps you stuck, too pessimistic about your own potential to muster the energy to start improving yourself. In contrast with this unproductive sort of self-blaming, self-compassion has been associated with success even when it comes to dieting to lose weight. My mother, as I think back, was a powerful model of self-compassion for me, from her early maintenance of those "restorative niches" I told you about in chapter 1 to the forgiving way she talked about herself. "I was not perfect and I made tons of mistakes, but I did the best I could at any given moment," she has told me.

In the wake of my unprecedented social success at Layton High School, I was not only able to be kinder to myself, I got better at tending to the relationships that were most important to me. This includes genuinely listening to my parents, who, as I finally recognized, had always had my best interests at heart. Suddenly I cared a lot more about what they thought, although of course I initially didn't let them know this. And as I paid more attention to them, it dawned on me how admirable they were. Had they always been that way? Or was I only now able to see it?

More impressive to me than anything either of them ever said was the way they had been living their lives, voting with their feet in favor of the value of education. This in fact is a common theme in the most positive relationships between parents and children: Good examples are always much more effective than words.

Many years later, after I'd gotten into Harvard, a reporter asked me what in the world had given me the confidence that I could go back to school after my previous failure. I realized I'd never actually thought about it in those terms. I'd watched both of my parents reinvent themselves by reeducating themselves, and seen how much they'd benefited. I only had to follow their footsteps. This is just one reason why dropping out of high school didn't ruin my future, as it sadly does for so many other kids. Once I decided to change, I had the foundation I needed to turn my life around.

Well before then, my parents had become models for me not only in respect to their career paths, but in how they were each growing as human beings. My father's career switch, which brought him so much more prestige and pay, to a surprising extent also seemed to make him more reflective and less reactive. As I saw it, he'd gone back to school as someone who could be quick to anger and emerged a model of self-control. As he gained self-respect, he seemed to be more able to worry less about me, and be a lot more patient, a development that was a powerful lesson for me, since I'd so long feared my own temper was beyond my ability to change. But here was my father, in his late forties, learning an entirely new way of handling his emotions. And if he could do it, maybe so could I.

Indeed, it was only once I moved out of my parents' house

that my dad and I started spending a lot more time together. Fortuitously, we'd both gotten interested in golf at the same time. We ended up meeting together almost every weekend, roaming the various golf courses of northern Utah, both of us walking and carrying our own clubs to save money. It was during these rambles that my dad began to dole out advice, and I realized that either he had gotten much smarter, or I'd grown up enough to recognize his wisdom.

My Dad, Redux

My father had always been strict, but never in a my-way-or-the-highway manner. I remember Kaylin's father, shortly after our marriage, warning me, "Never apologize to your children," advice that seemed so foreign to me after my own parents' more straightforward style. Particularly as my siblings and I grew older, both Larry and Lyda had made it a practice to own up to their mistakes and discuss them frankly.

One of my father's mantras was that everyone makes mistakes, but what truly builds and demonstrates good character is what you do afterward. This is particularly good advice for parents of kids like me, who make more than our share of gaffes. Rather than focus your energy on trying to stop the blunders, which is usually impossible anyway—at least in the short term—you can better help your child by encouraging him to be honest about what happened and to figure out what he can do to make things better.

My parents' approach helped inspire one of the smartest things

I did for myself during this time, which was to buy myself a small, black spiral notebook, in which I kept a log of the dumbest, most out-of-control things I did. I called it my "D'oh!" book, an homage to the cartoon character Homer Simpson. My teachers in religious school had encouraged me to write in a journal, but even as I finally took up this practice, it mortified me. What kind of loser needs to fill up a whole notebook with his stupid faux pas? Still, I was starting to recognize the usefulness of training my metacognition—the fancy word scientists use for the way you keep track of how you think and behave. Maybe if I flexed this mental muscle of self-control, I figured, I wouldn't keep throwing my golf clubs down after making a lousy shot. Maybe I wouldn't even have bought that Honda on my lunch hour. To ease the initial pain of this exercise—after all, this *was* one of my weakest muscles—I came up with the strategy of only allowing myself to read the book in times when my self-confidence was particularly high, like after I'd just hit a winning shot in a rec-league basketball game. At times like these, I was able to think over what had happened, determining if the error was truly to any degree my fault, and if so, what I could do about it. Usually I also included my dad's take on the incident, if he'd happened to witness it, or if, as was increasingly the case, I'd talked to him about it afterward.

There was the time, for example, when we were out golfing together, and my dad wandered off about twenty yards to look for his ball. I spotted him out on the fairway just as a woman in a short golf skirt walked in front of him. It struck me how funny it would be to wolf-whistle in her direction, making her think it was my dad. So of course I did just that. Had this been just two or three years ago, Larry might have (rightly) flipped out at my rudeness, and, conditioned as I was, I braced myself as he walked back to me. But instead, looking less angry than just slightly embarrassed, he quietly told me what a coincidence it was that he had just two weeks ago attended a sexual harassment training workshop at his job. "Son, I know you meant what you did as a joke, and I'm not saying it wasn't funny," he said. "But just imagine how that woman feels. A few minutes ago, she felt like a golfer. How does she feel now?" He then gave me a soft pat on the back and returned to his shot.

When I was growing up, my parents spent a lot of time arguing over the best way to raise me. Of the two, my father always seemed to have higher expectations, which he thought he could get me to fulfill with strict rules and consequences. He thought my mother was too soft, since she usually leaned more toward trying to build up my self-confidence, which she could see was below sea level. For various reasons, including sheer force of will, my mom routinely won these arguments, and I'm glad she did. When you've fallen into a hole, someone else's lofty expectations of you just aren't that helpful. Yet today I'm equally grateful for my dad's approach, which helped me enormously as soon as I was ready for it. This illustrates the point that there simply isn't one right way to raise a good kid. You can set all the goals you want starting out, but prepare to change your methods according to shifting circumstance. Once again, it's chess, not checkers.

At the same time, it's worth noting the abundant research demonstrating that children benefit more, in terms of mental health and general well-being, to the degree that both of their parents are involved, always assuming the involvement is benign.

Strong relationships between fathers and children have been linked with reduced risk of drug abuse, greater problem-solving ability, and even, interestingly enough, impulse control and memory.

Would a closer relationship with my dad earlier in my childhood have prevented me from misbehaving as a kid? I honestly don't know. Still, I'm certain that his guidance and example had a huge amount to do with the fact that I'm no longer working at jobs that bore me out of my mind.

As Larry and I started golfing together through the humid spring and summer of 1995, my son Austin's first year, I observed him and listened to him ever more closely. When he told me how hard it had been to return to school, I knew what he meant, having watched him take classes at night and on weekends on top of his full-time job. Yet I'd also witnessed, at close range, the rewards he'd earned, including more interesting work, more pay, a new house, and a lot more self-respect. I realized I wanted all those things, too, and pretty soon, I was forming a plan.

I'd taken a close enough look at myself by then (with the help of that "D'oh" journal) to know I wasn't lazy, but rather very easily bored, meaning that I wouldn't do well in the long run without more intellectually challenging work than stocking shelves or hawking cell phones. My dad had patiently explained, more than once, that I needed a lot more education before I could get that kind of a job. So I made up my mind that summer that I would return to school, as he had done, and that this time I'd make it count. I then proceeded to bask in this honorable newfound resolve, while doing nothing to act on it, for the next several months.

Back to School

I'd taken my GED exam within a couple of months after I'd dropped out of Layton High. Yet whenever the subject of the next logical step came up—that is, whether I'd continue my schooling, specifically by registering at the local college, Weber State—I always had some excuse for procrastinating. We couldn't afford the fees. I wouldn't have the time—after all, I was already so busy at my latest job, selling chain-link fence throughout the state, that I barely saw Kaylin and Austin during the week. Kaylin finally got fed up with me talking out of both sides of my mouth, and one morning while I was at work, borrowed some money from her parents and drove over to Weber State to sign me up for two night classes. The first of these was to begin the following Monday.

Kaylin chose the courses at random: Chemistry and English, as I recall. When I got home late that evening, she casually said, "You might want to go down to Weber and pick classes that you actually want before it's too late."

This was just the spur I needed to move forward, particularly after she told me the money she'd paid was nonrefundable. When I arrived at the registration office, however, I discovered that most of the classes were already full. What's more, even though Weber State theoretically offers open enrollment, the registrar informed me that my abysmal high school grades and test scores limited my eligibility for most classes. For the first year, I'd only be able to take courses offered off campus.

With such limited options, I managed to pick two classes that caught my interest: Economics 101 and Interpersonal Psychology. In choosing this way, I was heeding more of my father's good advice. It might have made sense to start out at Weber by getting the general requirements out of the way. But my dad had advised me to start out instead by taking classes that genuinely interested me.

"You don't have very good study skills," he had reminded me, as if I didn't already know it. "But your main problem is motivation. Pick classes you know you'll be interested in, and you'll figure out the study skills along the way."

I've had many occasions since that time to appreciate this timely advice. For me, the hardest part of learning always boils down to figuring out why I should care. Other people's expectations matter to me, but they rarely clinch the deal. I need to build up my own reasons to engage. But once I jump over that hurdle, I'm good to go.

I already knew that I cared about economics and psychology, not incidentally because both subjects were directly relevant to the trouble I was in during that transformational year. But by tremendous good fortune, I soon got another reason to care, in the form of Julianne Arbuckle, my psychology professor. From the first day of her class, I'd been determined to behave like a new person: a star student, who listens closely, nods sagely, and takes copious notes. To my delight, she treated me as if that was who I was. The two of us formed a thriving mutual admiration society that lasted right up until she assigned the first homework . . . and I failed to turn it in.

I'd reverted to my bad habits, choosing a two-night video game marathon with my brother over completing the assignment. Yet when Professor Arbuckle realized my homework was missing, she walked over to my desk with a look of concern.

"Todd, this isn't like you," she murmured.

"Lady, this is exactly like me," I wanted to answer, although, thankfully, I kept my mouth shut. She offered me one more day to complete the assignment, without penalty, and I realized I couldn't bear to disappoint her for a second time.

Then, a few weeks later, Arbuckle's apparently distorted image of me popped up again, after I'd skipped her evening class. It was my wedding anniversary, and I'd opted to take Kaylin to Salt Lake City for dinner, despite a raging snowstorm. Even so, a rather novel sensation—guilt—compelled me to try to make it back for the last part of the three-hour session. When I arrived, the class was empty except for just one of my classmates, who was reading her textbook at her desk. She looked up and asked me immediately if I was all right, adding, "Professor Arbuckle was so worried about you that she canceled class."

I paused to absorb this. My teacher had assumed that something terrible had happened to me—because, of course, I would have never skipped class without telling her in advance. Was this really possible, that someone could see me in this light? I accepted that it was and happily shouldered this new burden of living up to my teacher's image of me.

The Difference a Mentor Can Make

In subsequent years, and always with the memory of Professor Arbuckle in mind, I've been fascinated by the ongoing research into the importance of mentors not related by kin in young people's lives. There's a great deal of evidence that resilience is not, in fact, an inborn trait, as it has widely been assumed, but rather is the product of (you guessed it) a complex system involving a positive feedback loop, in which a child becomes strong at least in part due to other people's belief in him. Support for this perspective comes from a forty-year longitudinal study of 210 resilient children on the Hawaiian island of Kauai. Among other findings, the study showed that few of the children who turned out to be resilient had experienced prolonged separations from their primary caregiver during the first year of life; many were oldest children; none had a sibling born before they turned twelve; and all developed a close early bond with at least one caregiver, sometimes a grandmother, older sister, or other relative in the extended family.

"Resilience is not only an individual matter," writes the science journalist Katy Butler. "It is the outward and visible sign of a web of relationships and experiences that teach people mastery, doggedness, love, moral courage, and hope."

Parents can and so often do move mountains for their kids, as mine did for me, yet there comes a time when it is absolutely key for someone on the road to adulthood to earn the respect of another adult, who doesn't necessarily *have* to have faith in him. And although you can't manufacture such a relationship for your child, you *can* play an important supporting role by seeking out environments that lend themselves to this kind of interaction. Some situations, such as college, are ready-made for meeting mentors, but you needn't wait for your child to turn eighteen. Look for after-school sports or clubs or summer internships that provide lots of chances for older kids and adults to be role models.

Julianne Arbuckle played that vital role for me, teaching me that social expectations can work both ways. Back in middle school and high school, my teachers and fellow students got into the habit of expecting me to fail, making it easy to do so. But Professor Arbuckle, who saw me afresh, expected me to succeed, and that was all I needed, at that pivotal point in my life, to start doing so. For the first time in my life, I started asking myself what it would take for me to truly change my behavior, while also recognizing the need to manage my context to support this goal. (Incidentally, just to drive home the point about feedback loops turning small changes into big outcomes, I should say that when I graduated from Weber State, I told Professor Arbuckle about the defining role she had played, and guess what? She only vaguely remembered the interactions that were ultimately so meaningful to me.)

As part of my new context-management plan, I realized that I'd give myself my best chance of success by surrounding myself with other people who believed that I could succeed. I also knew that I needed a clean break from my past. So from that point on, I made it a rule to avoid any class where I'd run into someone from high school, someone who still thought of me as how I was then.

I also continued to take care in selecting my classes, cherry-picking only the ones with particularly engaging teachers, or material that was so interesting to me in itself that I trusted I'd stay the course. And, toward the end of my first year at Weber, I made another difficult, highly personal, and ultimately strategic decision that I know helped me reach my full potential. Nearly a decade after I was first prescribed stimulants to treat the symptoms associated with ADHD, I began to take them regularly.

Rethinking Ritalin

I'm going to digress for the next several paragraphs, given that the use of stimulants is, hands down, the most controversial topic in the field of attention and learning differences. And I certainly agree that it should be so. For one thing, every medication has side effects. (The most common downsides of stimulants are sleep problems, stunted growth, and cardiac risks for children with preexisting heart problems.)

Another important caveat is that stimulants are only one potential tool, and never a cure-all, for symptoms associated with ADHD. They don't work for everyone, even when side effects aren't a problem, and in any case, doctors report that most kids stop taking them after only about a year. This "lack of compliance," in what strikes me as rather Orwellian medical parlance, is normally ignored in debates about stimulants, yet is likely a major reason why federally sponsored researchers have found that opting to treat ADHD with stimulants on average doesn't reduce the risks of dire long-term outcomes for kids with this diagnosis.

Specifically, it won't, again on average, make kids more likely to graduate from school, avoid addiction to drugs and alcohol, and stay out of jail.

That's not to say that stimulants can't help certain people in certain contexts. For myself and many others, stimulants can help limit the extremes of impulsive and distractible behavior. Still, the limits of what they can do reflect one of the main points I've made throughout this book—namely, that behavior will always depend on much more than biology, altered or not.

I do realize that parents faced with the decision of whether to medicate a child have a more nerve-racking challenge than I did. You're taking on the responsibility for another person's developing brain, and you cannot take that burden lightly. I made my decision as an informed adult—so deliberately informed that I ended up taking a whole course in pharmacology at Harvard, where I wrote my term paper on the neural mechanisms of stimulants and their impact on cognition and behavior (and, incidentally, it's so boring you would need stimulants to read it). Among other things, my research reassured me of the safety of taking stimulants, despite the prevalence of wildly erroneous scare stories, usually circulating on the Internet, that would lead you to believe the drugs can cause cancer, depression, and other serious health problems. None of these alleged risks has empirical support, despite decades of research. At the same time, the choice of whether to medicate a child behooves parents to be keen-eyed detectives. There are so many ways to arrive at an ADHD diagnosis, and while research suggests the most common of these is via a family legacy (that is, genes), there are still many things a parent can manage in a child's environment, including diet and exercise, that can help reduce symptoms, sometimes to the point where medication isn't needed. Ideally—and even though it's a costly and time-consuming process—families should rule out other possible problems before giving medication to a child, especially since they can mask symptoms and make it seem like a problem has gone away even though it hasn't.

Once you are convinced that your child has a genuine learning or behavioral difficulty, you'll need to be a smart consumer when investigating potential treatments. Beware, in particular, of hucksters who tell you that your child has a "disorder" that can be "cured" with the help of a brain scan, a magnetic mattress, or any other usually expensive gimmick. But beware, just as much, of the hurried pediatrician who encourages you to try stimulants before ruling out other potentially helpful strategies.

As a young father juggling classes at Weber, I evaluated what I knew of the risks and benefits of stimulants and felt reassured that the balance was in my favor. Stimulants, as I've found, both by self-observation and research, are useful above all for one well-defined issue common to people like me. When we're not internally motivated to focus on something, we have to work a lot harder to stay on task in order to complete the work at hand. Midway through my first year at Weber, I could see it was taking me three or four nights to finish routine homework that other students could wrap up in a single evening, just by dint of their greater ability to keep their butts in their chairs. Whenever I'd get bored, it felt much too easy to wander off and play Nintendo, or read to Austin, or do any of an infinite number of more appealing things. So I looked to stimulants initially as a simple tool for a particular purpose—to help me finish assignments. In the process, I got into better study habits, which in time began to feel more natural to me.

I still take Ritalin today, despite some mixed feelings about it. Like most people, I want to believe that I'm in control of situations, and don't like the idea of sharing that control with a pill. On the other hand, I've come to see stimulants through a different lens, as merely one, albeit important, tool at my disposal—a way I've learned to help manage my environment to suit my particular brain.

Big Man on Campus

By my second year at Weber, my life had become a lot more challenging. Nathan, my youngest child, was born in 1996. Kaylin was taking care of the two kids full time, and money was tighter than ever.

I'd cut back my hours working off campus and applied for student loans so I could devote more time to study, although I also spent about ten hours a week working as a teaching assistant. The plan worked well: I'd become a straight-A student, now allowed to take all my classes on the main campus, and would graduate, two years later, with a 3.97 grade point average. This record earned me an academic scholarship, which paid for my tuition and books.

In all my classes, by this time, my teachers looked to me as one of their star students, and I behaved accordingly. I still occasionally blurted out comments in class, but, strangely enough, in this new context I was no longer seen as the annoying class clown but as this bright, creative person, full of ideas worth sharing. To this day I continue to be amused that some of the same behaviors that got me in such trouble in grade school could be seen by my college professors as so brilliant. On more than one occasion I was even told that my wit added so much to the class! It's one of the best examples I can think of for the rule that context matters.

I ran for and won a spot on the student senate, and went on to convince Weber's exclusive honors program to accept me as a member, meaning I could take advanced courses in a special building on campus. Not only did they let me in, but on graduating, I was named the honor student of the year.

While this was gratifying, what meant much more to me that year was the extraordinary empathy of a faculty member named Bill McVaugh, who noticed not only my academic record but how much I was struggling to keep my grades up and provide for my family. Without telling me, Professor McVaugh taught an extra course at the school to get funds that he used to hire me as a research assistant. That selfless act allowed me to quit my day job and focus harder on my studies.

Success bred success, and in the midst of it I discovered something I never would have believed for a minute back in high school. I actually enjoyed learning.

This revelation made me increasingly ambitious about my future. I wanted to continue with my education, going on to graduate school, and I knew just what I wanted to study: the science of learning itself, and what makes it easier or harder for people to achieve. Nothing I'd learned in my classes so far had resonated with my own experience. I was convinced there was a lot I might discover to help school be less of an endurance test for students like me.

Because no one in my family had ever attained more than an undergraduate degree, I realized that I needed some outside advice. I ended up interviewing several faculty members at Weber University about what they thought I should do. Eventually I decided to apply to no fewer than thirteen schools, a choice I didn't make lightly, considering the application fees. One of these was Harvard.

I never would have considered such a long-shot goal if I hadn't been encouraged by my mentor and advisor at Weber, Eric Amsel, chair of the psychology department. Professor Amsel was friends with a Harvard professor named Kurt Fischer, who had just become director of a new interdisciplinary venture, the first of its kind at the university, called Mind, Brain, and Education. Professor Fischer was known as a leader of a growing movement to apply biological and cognitive science to education. I researched his work and was excited by how much I shared his perspective and goals. And as I'd later discover, we had something else in common in our blue-collar childhood. Fischer's dad, the son of German immigrants, had been a salesman, truck driver, and vending machine technician. His son was the first member of his family to attend college in the United States. Unlike me, however, Fischer had had a positive experience in high school, which he attributes to a lucky break, when as a youth, he won a scholarship to a high-quality private school. When it came to mainstream public education, however, Professor Fischer and I shared a keen desire to help reform it.

Working with him would obviously be a dream, not least

because in the doctoral program, I'd have an unusual degree of independence and freedom to work in multiple disciplines. Still, I wondered if it was fair to Kaylin and the kids to risk the $120 application fee. As it was, we were all already eating much too much instant ramen.

I filled out the form, but about a month later, as I was sitting with Kaylin at my parents' kitchen table, I decided it was not worth the money, and dumped it into the garbage can. "I've got a much better chance at Michigan State," I told my family.

Shaking her head, Kaylin promptly retrieved the application from the trash and dusted off the pages. "There's nothing wrong with getting rejected, but if you don't even try, you're going to spend your life wondering what might have happened if you did," she told me.

A couple of weeks later, I got a thin envelope from Michigan State, containing a letter of rejection. But a few days after that, a fat envelope arrived from Harvard.

The news of my acceptance—this seemingly storybook ending to my earlier academic failure—was broadcast on Utah's ten o'clock TV news and made the front page of the *Salt Lake Tribune*. The newspaper featured a picture of Kaylin straightening my collar while my mom looks on. Kaylin and I are looking grim and focused, but my mom, who is wearing a gaily flowered dress, has her head thrown back in what looks like ecstasy. The caption says, "Todd Rose's mother says she always knew he would succeed."

BIG IDEAS
• • • • • • • • •

- As my father taught me, everyone makes mistakes, but what matters most is what you do next. I continue to believe that this is one of the most important things that you, as a parent, can teach your child.

- Having compassion for yourself is a prerequisite for healthy self-improvement. But keep in mind that it's not the same thing as letting yourself off the hook for bad behavior.

- Abundant research confirms the truth of what most people know intuitively, which is that children need their dads. Studies have shown benefits including a reduced risk of drug abuse, better impulse control, and even strengthened memory.

- Resilience isn't something you're born with, but rather is the result of positive feedback loops, most of which involve people who believe in you and provide their support.

ACTION ITEMS
▪ ▪ ▪ ▪ ▪ ▪ ▪ ▪ ▪ ▪ ▪ ▪

- Encourage self-awareness and self-compassion by keeping your own "D'oh" journal, recording your lapses of judgment so that you might later reflect on them. If you want to, share your insights with your child. My point is that before trying to understand your child, it's important that you understand yourself.
- Take a measured attitude toward stimulants for ADHD. The side effects aren't negligible and the pills are not a magic bullet. At the same time, under certain conditions, stimulants can be a useful tool in managing—not curing—impulsivity and distraction.
- Teach and help your child to find mentors throughout his or her life—all kids need adults outside their immediate families to help guide them.

· 8 ·

Failing Well

"Ever tried. Ever failed. No matter. Try again. Fail again.
Fail better."

—Samuel Beckett

Crash

The life of a square peg, by its very nature, is rarely distinguished by its stability. Predictability simply isn't our strong suit. Serenity tends to unnerve us. When the going gets too smooth, we may be counted on to roughen it up.

That said, and after thoroughly searching my self-doubting soul, I still can't find any reason to believe that I in any way invited the calamity that hit my family, literally, in the autumn of the year 2000, so soon after my triumph of getting admitted to Harvard. It began with an accident that ushered in one of the hardest years of my life, a phase I happily would have avoided if I'd had the choice, yet which ended up offering a valuable curriculum in the art of bouncing back. It happened only a few days after we arrived in Cambridge, Massachusetts, where Harvard is located. I had driven our minivan into a busy intersection, with Kaylin sitting next to me, and little Austin and Nathan in their car seats in the back. As I turned left, a woman driving a Toyota truck from the opposite direction ran through a red light and barreled into us, head-on. Our van skidded through the intersection and spun around. Just like in the movies, it seemed like it all happened in slow motion, and in complete silence.

As soon as the van stopped moving, Kaylin and I jumped out, and Kaylin slid the back door open to look at the kids. Austin, age six, got out on his own, but Nathan, two months shy of his fourth birthday, refused to unbuckle his booster seat. Instead he reached his arms out for Kaylin, who released him and picked him up. He wrapped his arms around her neck and stayed like that throughout the next two hours.

We stumbled over to sit on the curb, where a few passersby approached to ask if we were okay. The police and paramedics arrived within just a few minutes, but after checking briefly on us, went to help the Toyota driver, who hadn't left her truck and appeared to be seriously injured. The four of us sat in silence, while Nathan buried his head in Kaylin's chest, until the police said we could leave. The van—it wasn't even our van, but a loan from Kaylin's unluckily generous parents—was totaled, so we had to get a ride home in a squad car.

Back at the apartment, we once again asked the boys if they'd been hurt. Austin, whose arm was scratched and bleeding, said he was okay, but when Kaylin finally tried to put Nathan down, he screamed as if he were being stabbed.

Finally, he pointed to his thigh. As we'd soon discover, his right femur was fractured. We got a ride to the emergency room from our next-door neighbor, a graduate student whom we hadn't met until that evening, and ended up staying overnight at the Children's Hospital, where Nathan needed surgery.

For the next two months, poor Nathan had to wear a cast that covered nearly all of his body. To stabilize his hips, it went down from his chest to the toes of his right leg, and down to his knee on his left. Once the cast came off, he needed a full month of physical therapy to help him relearn how to walk.

Our medical bills amounted to roughly twenty thousand dollars, delivering the kind of unpredictable and devastating setback that, as I'd later learn, hits hundreds, if not thousands, of families every day in this country. What made it so much worse is that we had arrived from Utah betting on the come, as they say in the casinos, with our bank accounts depleted and with less than one hundred dollars in cash to last until my first student loan check. Under Massachusetts auto insurance regulations, we had to sue the Toyota driver to recover the bulk of our losses. The case lingered on for the next three years, during which I got into the habit of playing chicken with our bank account, often writing checks to pay our bills several days before my loan checks arrived, and simply paying the penalties when they bounced.

Throughout the next seven years that it took me to get my doctorate, I survived financially by taking out as many student loans as I could, while also earning extra cash as a teaching fellow. I juggled as many as five classes a week, and rarely slept more than five hours a night. Yet there was still never a month when we were able to pay all of our bills.

We had moved into a small, no-frills apartment that over-looked the building's trash bins. It smelled terrible all summer long, yet had the singular advantage of giving us dibs on valuables abandoned by our neighbors. Every piece of our furniture, from our bed to our kitchen table, was handed down by people who were moving out. Sometimes the transfer was made in person, but more often one of us would rush to nab a piece minutes after it was hauled out to the garbage.

Over all of these years, Kaylin managed the boys' schedules, homework, sports, and carpooling. She shouldered complete re-sponsibility for running our household, with all the thankless, unpaid, routine tasks that implies. This continued even after she got her first full-time job, at a child-care center near our apart-ment, and subsequently even after she went back to school her-self, eventually earning a master's degree in human development at Harvard.

Kaylin and I never explicitly negotiated this traditional divi-sion of labor. Perhaps, encouraged by our upbringing, we simply fell into roles that our own parents had filled. And of course I realize you might also suppose that Kaylin, who was far more or-ganized than I, and who gave me that critical push to register for college in the first place, was still, in addition to everything else on her plate, organizing *me*. By this point, however, she just didn't have time. Like so many other scrambling parents of young children, the two of us were lucky most days to get everyone out of the house in time for school and work. So, with Kaylin's or-ganizational bandwidth fully occupied, I had to sink or swim. For at least those first few years, I guess you could say I dog-paddled.

A Bad-Hair *Year*

As an additional budget-cutting move in those anxious weeks after the crash, I stopped going to the barber. Alas, my first effort to cut my own hair was such a comical failure that I ended up shaving most of it off. I showed up at our new-student orientation meeting looking like a skinhead, and not even a particularly tough one. Yet that wasn't the only reason I instantly felt out of place in the Eliot-Lyman room in Longfellow Hall, with its blue and gray walls, soaring ceilings, glass chandeliers, and gleaming oak table, around which the dozen of us new students sat on elegant, high-backed, uncomfortable wooden chairs.

As we took turns introducing ourselves, the student just before me went on for more than ten minutes, describing her stint at an elite prep school, followed by an undergraduate degree from Yale, and a year of "self-discovery" in Europe. After hearing this, I was so intimidated that when my turn came, I began by blurting out: "This isn't my usual haircut!" From there, I'm sure my fellow students' general perception of me deteriorated, especially given that just a few minutes later, after I somehow missed receiving a stack of materials that one of the faculty members was handing out, I piped up: "Would someone please pass the syllabuses?" This evoked a round of snickers, after which the over-privileged Yalie retorted: "You mean the *syllabi*?"

It made no difference, of course, that I was technically right about that arcane plural. The point was that I was way out of my Ivy League, and it seemed to me that everyone in the Eliot-Lyman room knew it. For the next couple of months, I struggled to put that awful first meeting out of my mind. I assured myself I'd have the last laugh, once I wowed my fellow students with my virtuoso academic performance. This confidence lasted right up until I got my grade on my first major assignment, a paper with the formidable title of "Information Processing and Central Conceptual Structures" for a course in "Cognitive and Symbolic Development," taught by the notoriously demanding professor Howard Gardner.

Professor Gardner is one of psychology's undisputed rock stars, famed in particular for his theory of "multiple intelligences," which suggests that the way psychologists and educators have traditionally defined intelligence is much too narrow, and as a result overlooks several important ways that kids can be smart. A child who can multiply numbers with ease, in other words, may be no more genuinely intelligent, nor more likely to succeed in life, than another who is gifted musically, spatially, or interpersonally.

I'd been fascinated by Gardner's work for years, writing one of my honors class term papers at Weber University on his theory. Despite his tough reputation—from the first day of school I heard rumors that his course is legendary for making unprepared students cry—I figured I had a good head start, and might even do well in his class.

My grade on that first paper was a C+.

At Harvard, a C+ is considered a failing grade.

My first thought was that Gardner's teaching assistant, an advanced doctoral student, had made a mistake. I was an A student, not a C student—or at least, I'd earned all A's back at Weber State University. But then I read Gardner's personal note, scribbled under the grade. I can still repeat it verbatim from memory. "Judging by your work here, it is not clear to me that you possess the writing skills to succeed at this level," he'd written.

I read the note over again, and then again, and again, feeling suddenly just as numb as if I were right back in that intersection, standing beside the wrecked minivan. I guess you could say I was in "flight" mode, since as soon as class ended I grabbed my books, blew off my next class, and headed for home.

My walk from the center of the campus to our apartment took about twenty minutes, passing under Harvard's famous flaming red- and orange-leafed elm trees and centuries-old redbrick dormitories that had once housed the likes of Emerson and Thoreau. Along the way, the numbness wore off, and I started to cry. My junior high school nightmare had finally come true. So many people had told me, for so many years, that I was so smart, and could do such great work if only I tried. And here I was, having tried my hardest, and failing. Maybe I really wasn't so smart after all.

Luckily I didn't run into anyone I knew, although that wasn't so surprising, since I knew so few people on campus. I had no one, in fact, that I felt able to confide in except for Kaylin, and given that she had left all of her family and friends to follow me on this now obviously doomed adventure, I couldn't imagine telling her what I was thinking—that we should catch the first plane back to Utah, lean on our parents again, and start over.

When I reached our building, I sat down on a wooden bench outside for about half an hour, contemplating my options. In a state of utter wretchedness, I fantasized for several minutes about how easy it would be to exploit Nathan's injuries to save my pride. Showing up back in Utah with our little boy all bandaged up might even make it look like I was being a good father, getting my family the support we needed rather than selfishly pursuing my career. I had my story ready for my mom, and walked over to a pay phone to call her. Luckily for me, however, nobody answered. I walked back to the bench, dried my eyes, and started thinking again.

That's when a memory popped into my head from a few months earlier, when I was still applying to graduate schools and interviewed at the University of California, Berkeley. It seems in retrospect like the timely redelivery of a gift I'd yet to open.

The Biggest Loser

My trip to California had been a powerful experience, not least because it was the first time I had ever flown in an airplane. Much like at the orientation meeting at Harvard, I felt like a hayseed compared to the dozen other recent graduates competing for a spot in the prestigious doctoral program, even granting that at that point I still had a decent haircut.

Throughout the day, we met with various faculty members who asked about our grades, goals, research interests, and why we thought Berkeley might be a good fit. I was ready for most of these questions, but repeatedly stumped by one. In every single interview, someone asked me to tell them about my biggest failure, and what I'd learned from it.

It was hard for me to believe that they really wanted me to answer this question honestly. Initially I assumed it was their way of weeding out the idiots willing to admit to their own stupidity, in which case it seemed that my best strategy was to find a faux-humble way to tell them about my strengths. *I care too much. I work too hard.* I tried that in the first interview, but after watching it bomb, switched at the next meeting to confessing I'd never finished my Eagle Scout project, a failure that supposedly taught me how important it is to finish things you start. This didn't go over any better. My interviewer's eyes appeared to be glazing over. So at my last meeting, I figured I had nothing to lose. "If you really want to know," I began, "my biggest failure is obvious. I flunked out of high school." This time the Berkeley interviewer sat forward in her chair, smiling eagerly. "That's interesting," she said. "Tell me more."

That evening, I ran into the same faculty member during a faculty-student reception. I managed to talk to her alone for a few minutes and finally asked her directly: was I the only one who had been asked that question, since everyone must have known about my dark history in high school? No, it turned out, that was pure paranoia. Instead, they had all come to agree that the answers to this particular question about failure were unusually predictive of future success. "As scholars, you're all going to need to be able to deal with adversity," she told me, "and grades don't tell us anything about that. What we need to know is how honest you were about where you went wrong when you had trouble, and how you used that to move forward."

As I sat and pondered this memory in Cambridge, in the cool of that early autumn twilight, I realized a few things. Above all, there was no way I was going to take that flight back to Utah. Not only did I know how much it would have hurt to quit, but what if someone at some future interview once again asked about my biggest failure? Would I have to acknowledge that I'd risen beyond my potential, that I didn't really have what it took to survive at Harvard, and that I couldn't bear to be criticized? Besides, after all of last summer's hoopla in the press, how would I ever live that down? How would my mom?

Confronting myself this way helped me remember what my father had told me so many times while we were golfing together: that everyone makes mistakes—some, like me, certainly more than others—but what matters most is what you do next. Getting that bad grade because I hadn't sufficiently prepared for Gardner's course was an error that was definitely worthy of the "D'oh!" journal I had kept during my years at Weber State University. But now the stakes were higher and I needed to do more to make amends. I promised myself that I would try harder from then on not to be so surprised and flustered by setbacks, but rather to use each one as a lesson on how to move forward.

Failing Better

Just as that Berkeley professor suggested, there is research supporting the idea that the ability to "fail well"—staying calm despite adversity, and making the most of experience learned through mistakes—predicts success in a variety of professional fields. Silicon Valley entrepreneurs frequently recite the mantra "Fail early and often," acknowledging the obvious truth that never failing suggests you haven't really tried. Howard Gardner himself has commented on this phenomenon, writing, in his 1998 book, *Extraordinary Minds*, that high-achieving people share "a special talent for identifying their own strengths and weaknesses, for accurately analyzing the events of their own lives, and for converting into future successes those inevitable setbacks that mark every life."

Still, while many people intuitively grasp that failure is not only part of learning but also can help lead to long-term success, what's harder to appreciate is why so many of us have trouble failing well. Part of the problem surely has to do with the prevalent human habit of denial. It's sometimes so painful to accept unwelcome information that our brains literally prevent us from recognizing it.

Now, denial may sometimes be a useful habit of mind, at least in the evolutionary sense—like when it comes to people deciding to have a baby even after observing their friends' teenagers. In most cases, however, it's usually worthwhile to recognize the habit and develop ways to open your mind to information even when it makes you uncomfortable. Otherwise you may easily miss learning something useful.

Legends are told about the many great discoveries that came to us by accident. From penicillin to Post-it notes, Popsicles to the microwave, a lot of things we take for granted today first snuck into view when people were looking for something else. A big reason we celebrate these accidents so enthusiastically may be our underlying awareness of how hard it is to accept the unexpected.

Consider the case of a large group of Stanford University biochemists who were closely observed in the 1990s by the social sciences researcher Kevin Dunbar. After monitoring four of the biochemists' labs, Dunbar was able to document that more than 50 percent of the data collected was notably different from what the scientists had expected. It wasn't uncommon for the researchers to spend as long as a month on a project and then discard the data because the findings didn't seem to make sense. When results didn't square with their initial hypotheses, they routinely at first suspected they had made a mistake, or used the wrong methods, and needed to try the experiment once again. Sometimes they even rejected information that appeared consistently, in multiple trials.

Dunbar began to worry about this. What possibly useful information—what new varieties of penicillin or Post-its—might these excellent scientists be chucking overboard? The problem with science, he suspected, wasn't the number of experiments that failed, but the tendency to ignore all the products of those failures.

Whyever would successful scientists at one of America's most prestigious institutions behave in such a self-defeating way?

The problem is at least partly biological, stemming from what you have learned (in chapter 3) is the highly variable capacity for perception.

Over the past few decades, brain scientists have found that, to varying degrees, we humans selectively (and habitually) edit what we learn through our senses, normally welcoming new data that substantiate what we think we already know, while often overlooking information that appears to contradict our beliefs. Researchers who study brain scans believe they have identified the culprit in this regard: the dorsolateral prefrontal cortex, located just behind the forehead. Oversimplification is always a risk when you write about brain regions being "responsible" for something or other, so it's best to say that this brain area is known to play an important role, together with other parts of the brain, in suppressing unwelcome bits of reality.

Compounding all this is the role of the stress hormone cortisol, which, as I told you about in chapter 4, can sabotage clear thinking. Learning from mistakes is a highly demanding mental process, requiring the capacity to reflect coolly on your immediate experience, comparing it to what you had expected, and also to imagine alternatives. Yet when most people make mistakes, it triggers a cortisol release, thwarting short-term memory in particular, and making all of those mental tasks much harder, especially in people who are already anxious. Instead we may be diverted by thoughts of catastrophe (I'm a failure! I'm going to get fired! My family will be homeless!) or alternative explanations that fit with our established beliefs by absolving us of responsibility. (Roscoe forgot to wash the beakers again!) In short, on these occasions, when you need all your mental powers most—to learn from failure—you're also at an unusually high risk of losing them.

In the case of the Stanford scientists, it's likely that these biological factors were at play—combined with a strong cultural influence. They didn't get their prestigious positions by being lousy students in grade school, which suggests that they'd trained in a system that explicitly teaches us that failure is not an option.

Despite a lot of routine talk by educators about the value of learning from mistakes, the truth is that we are very far from practicing what we preach in schools. In fact, the way students are taught and tested throughout America most emphatically gives the opposite message. The powerful lesson that young minds learn from our school system is that failure betrays an innate deficiency in the person who is failing, and it should be avoided at all cost.

This kind of instruction is not helpful for any child, but I think it's particularly damaging for the kind of kid that I was then: one bound to make more than his share of embarrassing errors. Rather than being taught to "lean in" to such errors to learn from them, students more often learn to try to cover their tracks, even if that means lying or blaming other people—habits guaranteed to prevent any chance that a boneheaded mistake may lead to someplace fruitful.

The Trouble with Billy

I witnessed a vivid example of this sad state of affairs during a visit to a third-grade classroom in a southern U.S. city I'm not at liberty to name, due to the protocols of the research. I'd gone there with my colleague Gabrielle Rappolt-Schlichtmann to field-test a prototype of a new learning software program that she had helped design, based on notebooks that students have to keep in science class. I'll tell you more about this digital notebook in the Epilogue, but basically it's a high-tech way of helping a wide variety of students to study science by presenting material in lots of different ways, while offering supports to help develop skills such as note-taking, making predictions, and learning from wrong guesses.

In the classroom we visited, we researchers stood at the

blackboard while the teacher and her aide introduced us and explained why we were there.

"Scientists love mistakes!" the teacher began. "That's how they learn. They test what are called hypotheses, and each time one doesn't work, they learn how to improve the next one." Scientists use their mistakes to get smarter, she told the class. "Who's ever made a mistake?" she asked the class. Hands shot up, slowly at first, but eventually every kid's hand was in the air.

"Me too," said the teacher. "And I don't like to make them, but I try to learn from them." She concluded her pep talk to the students by saying, "In our class, don't you think we should try and be more like scientists?"

This is perfect, I thought, as I smiled at the teacher. But at that moment, a movement in the back of the room drew my attention to a wiry, disheveled-looking boy I'll call Billy, whose behavior I immediately recognized. He was sitting at his desk, unable to keep still, kicking his shoes off and then spinning the mouse on his computer around. The soles of his shoes were all worn down, just like mine had been at his age. It was the telltale sign of a restless troublemaker.

And, sure enough, five minutes into our test, one of Billy's wandering fingers hit the "back" button on the browser of the new software, which, unpredictably, crashed the system.

It was soon clear to everyone in the room who was to blame. Billy's face turned vermilion as he looked down at his stockinged feet and made small ducking motions, as if trying to figure out if he could hide under his desk. The students groaned, while Billy's teacher and her aide shot him dark looks. This wasn't the first time poor Billy had interrupted their routine.

My colleagues and I exchanged a glance. We understood right away that Billy had done us a great service, justifying our trip to the school. The issue with the "back" button was an obvious problem—although it hadn't been obvious to us until then. If Billy hadn't inadvertently alerted us to it, someone else surely would have, down the line, and maybe at a much greater cost.

Fortunately, we were able to explain this to Billy's teacher and classmates in a way that seemed to get through. Billy wasn't punished, and for the next three weeks the class devoted itself to finding other "bugs" in our system.

As that day in the third-grade classroom suggests, one reason we all deal so poorly with mistakes must certainly be that, in so many cases, they're a sign that we need to do more work, both physically and neurologically. Seen in the most positive light, the immediate aftermath of any error is a sweet spot, where all kinds of learning and growth can take place. That said, however, it also requires extra energy. After Billy's mistake, my colleagues and I had to spend time correcting the "bug" he'd discovered. Similarly, my C+ from Professor Gardner, several years earlier, pushed me to spend scores of hours I had never thought I would have time for doing catch-up work I hadn't known I'd needed.

What buoyed me all through this process is a self-compassionate strategy known as reframing, which in this case refers to the art of talking to yourself about embarrassing adversity in a more positive light. In this case, it meant I had to reinterpret Professor Gardner's comments about my writing as his way of telling me not that I was a useless failure but that I simply needed a bit of remedial work.

Fortunately for me, I had learned about the magic of reframing through a previous mistake I'd made, back at Weber State University. At the time, I was working as a research assistant for my beloved mentor, Bill McVaugh. He had given me a data set that he told me he wanted me to analyze using a statistical technique called principal component analysis. I had no idea what principal component analysis was, but assumed I was supposed to be adept at it, because otherwise why would he have given me the job? So, under that assumption, I tried to fake my way through the work. When Professor McVaugh saw my results, he called me into his office and began by saying something on the order of "I should have realized that you couldn't do this." Those words set my teeth on edge and immediately caused me to argue and make excuses.

McVaugh, who, fortunately for me, was unusually patient and wise, didn't argue back, but instead called for a halt, during which he explained that language is always imprecise, and that it was important for me to be open to multiple meanings, rather than automatically assuming the worst. What he had meant to tell me, he said, was that he should've realized I couldn't do that kind of analysis, not because I wasn't smart, but because Weber State had no courses that taught the method. Once I applied McVaugh's principle to Gardner's feedback, my next step was obvious. It was time to improve my writing. Over the next few days, I checked around on Harvard's website and found that each department offered a free writing lab for its students. This made it clear that not only was I not alone in needing help, but that help was readily available. All I had to do was shed my pride and ask for it.

I went ahead and shed it—or at least some of it. I decided against taking the support offered by the writing lab in my own department, in favor of the relative anonymity of a workshop for undergraduates. The tutor, an undergrad student herself, turned out to be an exceptionally talented writer and teacher. Over the rest of the semester, I reported to her once a week to talk about my writing, to show her first drafts, and get tougher about taking criticism. She taught me that writing itself is a process of learning from mistakes. Very few writers produce polished prose in their first drafts. Just as with science experiments, the best writing is usually the product of many trials and errors.

My story's happily-ever-after ending is that I recovered from the disastrous first paper and got an A in Gardner's class. That was all the reward that I needed to convince me that this approach to failure was as useful as it was painful.

A Leading National Expert on Me

In the years since I bounced back from dropping out of high school, I've often been told that I am unusually "resilient." While I appreciate the compliment, I have to say that I dislike this word just as much as I dislike other labels we use with kids. In the case of this one, it strikes me a lot like someone going to a racetrack and picking a winner—after the end of the race. Resilience isn't something a child has from birth, as is often implied, but more something that's acquired. It wasn't the reason I got to where I am today. Instead, I gradually *became* resilient both because of the sum of my experiences, which helped me acquire an unusual amount of self-knowledge, and because I had support from others when it mattered the most.

By the time I arrived in Cambridge, for instance, I had recognized that one of my "interesting variabilities" is impulsivity—meaning I'm a lot more prone than most other people I know to say or do something I'll later regret, particularly in contexts where I am stressed out or otherwise emotionally charged. Yet because I'm convinced that impulsivity can have its advantages, I set out to manage it rather than try to "cure" it, making the most of the upside while minimizing the chance that one silly act or word might cause me or others irreparable harm. By remembering that context is key, I can at least try to anticipate when and where I'm likely to have problems, and plan accordingly, even if it means simply giving myself a little heads-up talk ahead of time.

I do this, for example, almost every time I walk on my way home from work past the gorgeous glass windows of an elegant restaurant called Harvest, which is tucked away under the linden trees in Harvard Square. Without fail, something about the fancy suits inside, and the lobsters being served, and the earth tones of the walls, and the outdoor heaters so the patrons don't get chilled, all converge to bring out the troublemaker in me—and, I swear to you, it's all I can do to stop myself from banging on the windows just to startle the rich people feasting inside.

Now, over the years I've examined this childish impulse far more times than any reasonable person should, wondering why this instinct is so strong, and warning myself just how stupid I'd look if I gave in to it. (After all, even I know that Harvard faculty members do *not* ordinarily bang on restaurant windows!) So far, this mature deliberation has kept me from following my heart. Still, whenever I'm in a really bad mood, or I know I'm particularly tired, I take care to choose another route home.

A similar, if more adult-like calculation leads me to be hyper-cautious (compared to my peers) about the time I might spend using social media such as Facebook or Twitter. Don't get me wrong; I love these tools, and I really wish I could spend more time interacting with family and friends. However, I also recognize that these are inordinately dangerous places for someone like me, not so much for the time I could waste, but because of the absence of a delete button that might save me from making some off-the-cuff remark that could dog me throughout my career.

In the nonvirtual world, meanwhile, I've somewhat similarly trained myself to notice early signs of a problem and remove myself from situations—for instance, with relatives, friends, or colleagues—in which I'm feeling angry or disrespected, on the understanding that I need time to give myself a chance to think reasonably. I also try to follow this practice whenever I make mistakes, with other people or in my work, as of course I continue to do. I'm not great at it, but I keep trying.

The bottom line is that it's not as if I've managed to extinguish all the feelings of anger, sadness, shame, self-blame, and fear, which still reliably arise whenever I do something dumb—and much less that I've actually stopped doing dumb things. Nor am I convinced that I'd want to, since sometimes such feelings can be helpful. The difference is that I'm more prepared to cope with them when they do arise, and to remind myself, as often as I need to, that any one behavior or mistake does not define me.

Strategies and Tools

Besides helping to keep me out of at least some kinds of trouble, becoming aware of my particular strengths and weaknesses and how they play out in different contexts has helped me deal more effectively with information demands and, as a result, has helped me become more organized and productive. Remember how I told you about my appallingly weak working memory? Well, to survive at Weber State, and of course also at Harvard, I realized that I needed to build a system to compensate for it. Believe it or not, I relied for several years on writing my most important reminders on my hand. That was right up until a day in 2006 when I happened to share an elevator ride with my statistics professor, a teacher I particularly respected. She caught sight of what I used to call my "organizational tattoos" and snickered, "How *old* are you, Todd?"

From that point on, I determined to refine my self-management strategies, a quest no doubt aided by the fact that at the time I was focusing my research, and writing my dissertation, on the topic of working memory. In the process, I've been able to investigate what sorts of systems best meet my needs, and, by extension, those of millions of other people like me who may be having some trouble remembering what you just said.

One of the main things I've learned is how important it is for me to be able immediately to "capture" new information, rather than letting it float in the nether regions of my awareness, making me anxious as I keep trying to remember just what it was that I needed to do. This phenomenon is actually so prevalent that cognitive scientists have a special term for it: "open loops"—an image suggesting a nagging need for closure. To close those loops and keep my focus clear of pestering worries, I've programmed my cell phone, laptop, and desktop at home so that wherever I am, I can make a note that will be immediately available in all three places. This simple practice frees my mind to go on to the next task.

I have also learned to use technology to protect me against some of the risks posed by technology. Having recognized that my extraordinary love of novelty puts me at risk of going off on endless Google-powered information-hunting expeditions, even as work deadlines fly past, I've programmed my desktop's browser to raise a flag after I've spent fifteen minutes surfing. It's just as likely that I'll ignore as heed that flag, but I like having the opportunity to choose whether I will keep surfing or get back to work. For people who need even more help, there are now computer programs that shut off your access to e-mail and the Internet for blocks of time, unless you reboot your computer.

To help me stay on track with errands and projects, I rely on an organizational system based on insights from one of my favorite books—*Getting Things Done*—written by the productivity guru David Allen. I implement my organizational system with a software program that organizes my projects and tasks and reminds me of approaching deadlines. One big advantage of this kind of organizational system is that it has taught me how to break down big projects into much less overwhelming tasks. I have trained myself to set aside the first fifteen minutes of every morning to make sure my system is on track, and I usually dedicate an hour on Sundays to updating it.

In all these ways and more, I "offload" demands and automate mundane tasks, making them manageable and in the process freeing up my working memory for more meaningful work. The benefits have extended far beyond increasing my productivity. Once I created a system I trusted to help me manage my open loops, my stress level dropped considerably and I found it much easier to sleep at night. As our information culture inexorably gets more demanding, and the options for where to focus our attention explode, I predict many people with supposedly excellent working memory will have to rely on similar systems.

Positive Feedback Loops

As my strategies and tools have helped me get more done, my self-confidence has improved, and I've been able to achieve even more. I got my doctorate from Harvard in 2007, and tried not to mind that instead of a diploma at the graduation ceremony, I was given a notice reminding me that I owed the university another $6,500. (I got the diploma once I paid that bill.) I went on to a postdoctoral fellowship at the Smithsonian Center for Astrophysics, and I am now a faculty member at the Harvard University Graduate School of Education.

Today I have the privilege of collaborating with an extraordinary group of colleagues from throughout the world. To be sure, I'm still paying off what at last count was $180,000 in student loans (and which, of course, was worth every penny). Meanwhile, I often reminisce with my mother, who, with all of her five kids now more or less off on their own, is indulging her own restless nature as never before, plotting overseas adventures that liven up her routine of a three-day-a-week nursing job combined with taking care of her own aging mom and her grandkids. Once or twice a year, she goes on missions with Operation Smile, which sponsors reconstructive surgeries for underprivileged children. So far she has traveled to India, China, Thailand, Ecuador, and the Philippines. "I try to enjoy each stage of life, but I must admit this one is pretty great," she says. She applauds my successes but has often teased me about what she has called the injustice of the fact that my two sons, now teenagers, have been models of good behavior. (If she only knew!)

My life's peaks and valleys, and the wisdom that my parents and all my other generous mentors so skillfully helped me gain, continue to inform my professional work, which focuses on re-imagining learning through the lens of complex systems. There are mornings on which I'll awake from dreams of being back in middle school, once again as the pitiable square peg doing the Devil's work of challenging authority, and need to remind myself that I am now the witty lecturer who spurs innovation by questioning conventional assumptions. Each time I consider this contrast, I marvel anew at the power of context.

Because, after all, I'm still the same person.

BIG IDEAS
• ■ • ■ • ■ ■ • ■

- The Merriam-Webster online dictionary accepts either *syllabi* or *syllabuses* as the plural of "syllabus."

- Failing well—that is, staying calm through adversity and recognizing what can be learned from mistakes—is a foundation of success in a variety of fields.

- Penicillin, Popsicles, the microwave, and superglue were all discovered by accident.

- Many scientific experiments fail—but the greater risk is that the value of many of those failures is ignored.

- To learn from mistakes takes an unusual level of mental capacity and effort. The emotional experience of failure can swamp the brain in stress hormones and interfere with clear thinking.

- In the information age, we all need a system to expand our working memory.

ACTION ITEMS
● ▪ ▪ ● ▪ ● ▪ ● ▪ ● ▪ ▪ ●

▪ Develop your own system to extend your natural cognitive abilities and to help you stay organized and productive. I suggest you start by testing existing approaches, such as those recommended in *Getting Things Done,* and see what works (and what doesn't) for your particular kind of variability. Teach your kids to follow suit.

By the way, among the specific technologies I've found helpful to increase my productivity are:

▪ "Things," a Mac task management system that helps me prioritize my goals and break down big jobs into little ones; it also keeps track of pending errands.

▪ A similar task management tool called "OmniFocus" goes one step further, reminding me of chores I need to do whenever it is convenient to do them. For instance, if I need to mail a letter, the program will make my smartphone vibrate to alert me if I'm within three miles of a post office.

▪ "Freedom," a downloadable software program, shuts off your access to e-mail and the Internet for a designated time, letting you sustain attention to a task at hand.

Creating New Contexts for Learning

"If we teach today as we taught yesterday, we rob our
children of tomorrow."

— JOHN DEWEY

Education Gets Personal

A couple of years ago, I watched a child's future change course,
all because of a new digital software program.

I was visiting a fourth-grade public school science class with
two of my colleagues, field-testing the Internet-based science
notebook I first mentioned in chapter 8. A few minutes after the
teacher introduced us, she called our attention to a gangly, quiet
boy named Dan, who had been diagnosed with dyslexia. Dan had
been struggling in all of his classes, which was all the more the
pity, said his teacher, since she had noticed that he had what she
called "a scientist's mind." Inquisitive, imaginative, and persistent,
he was nonetheless stalled at the classroom's starting gate by his
troubles with reading and organizing his thoughts. If his school
career continued like this for much longer, it was hard to imagine him enduring for many more years. What's more, it was a

good bet that Dan wasn't the only square peg in that class—there may well have been one or two or several other potential science stars in danger of getting left behind by the teach-to-the-middle constraints.

The technology that we developed for Dan's class helped him—and his fellow students—in several important ways. Among other things, it came with a built-in, text-to-speech feature, as well as headphones, offering the option of listening to the text instead of reading it. Dan and his classmates could also see material represented in a variety of ways, with pictures, videos, and graphs all raising the chances of information sinking in. Similarly, the program offered students multiple ways of demonstrating what they had learned. Rather than relying strictly on handwritten notes, anyone who chose to could type, draw, create audio recordings, or upload images and diagrams. Not least, shy students—including Dan—could now communicate directly with their teacher via an e-mail program embedded in the software, giving these learners a channel for timely feedback, while sparing them the embarrassment of needing to raise their hands continually during class.

Dan adapted quickly to the new system and within a few weeks, as his teacher happily informed us, he seemed like a different kid. Her insight proved true: He had a natural aptitude for science, which he could now finally demonstrate. His confidence grew with each new achievement, and he soon became the go-to guy for other students who had questions it seemed that only Dan could answer.

I can't think of a better example of Aristotle's principle of "unimpeded excellence" than the story of Dan with his science notebook. It strikes me as the perfect harbinger of a new, technology-enabled approach to education, one capable of vastly improving the lives of millions of currently frustrated children, parents, and teachers. It's important to remember, however, that it wasn't just the software that changed Dan's classroom experience, but a new way of looking at kids like him, within schools and in families, with a new appreciation for the hidden gems these square pegs have to offer.

You know all about my narrow escape from both conventional schooling and a lifelong alienation from learning. My aim now is to give you a glimpse of the kinds of projects being launched today—including some in which I'm personally involved—which I believe offer hope for similarly imperiled bright young minds.

We're living at a moment of unprecedented opportunity in American education, brought to us by a convergence of two dramatic trends—technological innovation and economic necessity. Seizing this moment as it deserves would mean reinventing education as we've known it for much too long, creating new contexts in which schools become places of rigor, relevance, and promise for *all* students. The danger, of course, is that this very same convergence could just as easily lead to a dismal situation in which warm-blooded mentors are replaced with computers, and school becomes *more* rather than less like factories.

I'll tell you more about that danger as well. But for the moment, let's get back to Dan, and his high-tech science notebook.

The software's arrival could not have been timelier for Dan and his classmates, who to one degree or another were all trying to match a unique array of strengths and weaknesses to a cookie-cutter education delivery model. Along with fourth graders throughout the United States, the class we visited was just beginning to study science in a serious way: observing experiments, collecting and analyzing data, drawing conclusions, and writing up reports. That's a daunting set of high-order thinking demands for most students, and too often, it's simply beyond the grasp of kids who are already falling behind.

The notebook is a particularly ambitious example of technology that frees students from the trap of conventional educational contexts that ignore natural learning variability. For students with poor working memory (like me), for instance, it offers "just-in-time" instructions as these learners complete their tasks, so they aren't overwhelmed by trying to remember every step. When they sit down to write up their results, they get reminders about how to proceed, with tips, for example, on what a good first sentence should include. Children who have trouble staying organized can rely on to-do lists, which break down projects into small pieces, giving them valuable practice in a key skill. Students who are still learning English can mouse-click on unfamiliar words to have them defined.

My colleagues have since tested this device with hundreds of kids in urban, low-income schools and have confirmed that it improves academic performance. It's no wonder that my friend Tim Blair, a San Francisco college student who struggled all the way through grade school—much like I did—compares these new technologies to Batman's secret weapon: his high-tech utility belt. "It makes no difference that Batman doesn't have any superpowers," Blair says, "as long as he's got that belt." While I like that analogy, I also have a more prosaic image of the notebook: a bulldozer removing obstacles in the wake of superpowers kids already have.

Blair, who talks nearly as fast as I do, and whose wiry build and frizzy hair reminds me of the cartoon character Sideshow

Bob, on *The Simpsons,* knows what he's talking about. Diagnosed with ADHD in kindergarten, he switched schools five times before his senior year in high school, mostly due to discipline and social problems, and eventually became an advocate for other kids like him, through a San Francisco–based group called SAFE Voices. One of his earliest memories of school is being sent, in tears, to the principal's office in third grade because he wouldn't show his math work. "Teachers used to tell me I was going to prison," Blair recalls today. "Not that I *would* go if I kept up some behavior, but that I *was* going." The right high-tech support, as well as a lot more understanding from humans, might have prevented some of that misery, Blair says, although he adds that the tool he's really waiting for is a "remote control device that could fast-forward, rewind, or eject your teacher."

Education reformers refer to the magic that inspires Tim Blair and that brought out the scientist in Dan as *personalization*—by which they mean a quest to use the power of digital technologies to transform our current cookie-cutter curriculum to meet the needs of many more students. At this writing, the increasing adoption of digital technology is clearing the way for similar miracles in thousands of schools throughout the nation, ushering in a long-overdue revolution. In fact, it's all happening at such an accelerating rate that I'd give the printed textbook another five years of life at best.

Now I like speed as well as the next guy born with an extremely low tolerance for boredom, but in this case we need to move forward thoughtfully. Economic necessity can be a powerful motivator for doing the hard work necessary to produce meaningful and lasting change; it can also be an excuse for taking shortcuts, such as giving the number crunchers leeway to cut costs by trying to automate education, laying off teachers even as they invest in computers. This trend might easily lead to a state of affairs in which, in the words of education historian Diane Ravitch, "the poor will get computers [and] the rich will get computers and teachers."

We simply can't let that happen, given all that we know now, including, I hope, what you've learned from this book about the power of complex systems in human behavior. I'm referring here specifically to the impact of emotions and context and the power of feedback loops when it comes to learning, including the transformative potential of adult mentors in the lives of square-peg students. Nonetheless, we can't let our fears delay us from offering utility belts (or bulldozers) to kids like Dan and Tim—not the least because, whether we like it or not, the wiring of U.S. schools is inevitable.

Learning Unleashed

U.S. classrooms have been plugging into new educational technology at a dizzying rate. Strategies that began in a limited way mostly to help homeschoolers are rapidly becoming mainstream classroom staples. In the decade beginning with the year 2000, the number of K–12-grade students taking an online course shot up from 45,000 to 4 million. At this writing, more than half a million grade school students now attend online schools full time.

As I've visited schools throughout the United States in recent years, I've been delighted to discover many ways in which this digital wave in education, combined—and this is key—with new understanding about the variability in how people learn, has been liberating students like Dan and Tim Blair from the miseries of educational contexts that ignore their variability. Already, thousands of U.S. schools have been incorporating cutting-edge tools to customize instruction in ways that help students embrace learning as never before. Many of them are claiming significant progress in student achievement, without spending any more, or even at reduced cost. What I find especially exciting about this trend is that the progress hasn't been limited to private or charter schools; it has been slowly influencing many mainstream public schools as well. One reason for this is the new economic reality of education, in which public school districts are essentially being forced to modernize, as they pare their budgets.

That budget pressure helps explain why one of the boldest experiments to date at this writing, a pilot project known as the School of One, was born in the New York public school system. The pioneering program is intended not only to make school a lot more engaging and helpful for all kinds of students, but also, eventually, to save money on books, paper, and personnel.

With the help of a sophisticated computerized system, School of One students follow individualized lesson plans, which are produced each day anew, based on what and how these learners did the day before. Each morning, the children report to a wall of computer monitors that resemble an airport's arrival and departure screens, where they learn their daily schedules. Depending on their ability to move forward, or their need to review, they then proceed either to hands-on group activities, computer sessions, or individual instruction. Kids learn at their own paces, and, ideally, in ways that suit each of them best. No one gets held back or pushed forward.

While it's still too early to assume that the School of One model is the wave of the future for U.S. education, it's hard to ignore its achievements when it comes to standardized tests. In 2009, a School of One pilot project reported that it had raised middle school students' scores by 28 percent, a remarkably rare impact. And elsewhere in the country, other tech-heavy experiments are reporting similar rates of success, particularly with students in low-income communities. In San Jose, California, a small charter school network called Rocketship Education, founded in 2007, has quickly risen to become one of California's top-performing schools for students living in poverty. And in Colorado, DSST Public Schools, a charter named for its flagship, the Denver School of Science and Technology, claims similar wonders with low-income students, reporting that every single one of its graduates has been accepted to four-year colleges.

The managers of these new ventures are driven by an awareness that our nineteenth-century Prussian education system is neither adequately engaging the majority of students nor preparing them for a world so recently transformed by an instant and endless supply of information. Among the most obvious measures of that failure is the high U.S. rate of high school dropouts that I told you about in the Prologue, plus recent data revealing that close to half of all students entering college quit before getting their diploma. America's rapidly declining rate of college grads, compared to other nations, helps explain why many leading U.S. firms have been going abroad to fill high-paying jobs in science, engineering, and computer programming. Modernizing our education system simply must be a priority, in other words, if we want to remain competitive in the globalized, digitized, twenty-first-century economy.

High-tech Highs and Lows

Here's what I see as the game-changer in this grand scenario: by the end of the first decade of the new millennium, the prices of software and computing devices, such as the iPad, finally fell to a point where they were competitive with textbooks. That simple change has been transforming the consciousness of government bureaucrats and entrepreneurs alike.

For example, in 2009, when then-California governor Arnold Schwarzenegger revealed this country's first state-sponsored plan to develop e-textbooks for high school math and science classes, he promoted the high-tech upgrade as a *budget-cutting* move. Whereas once schools had to argue for extra funds for computers and software, the idea now was that these digital books would help substitute free, open-source content for increasingly expensive, quickly outdated texts that have been weighing down both students' backpacks and state coffers for too long.

Schwarzenegger's switch put the old-fashioned publishing industry on notice, while firing the enthusiasm of a new class of e-entrepreneurs. California had been spending nearly $400 million a year on textbooks—a chunk of change that can inspire a lot of innovation. And, as no surprise, several of California's Silicon Valley corporate titans, including people with experience at companies like Google and Facebook, are starting to lead the evolving global market in e-education. Nonprofit ventures are also pushing the digital education envelope. In Palo Alto, California, the C-K12 Foundation has pioneered an open-content, Web-based collaborative "Flexbook," with which it hopes to reduce costs of textbooks throughout the world. In 2010, the foundation partnered with NASA to produce an innovative physics textbook.

At this writing, several states have been following California in transitioning to e-books. Even my own home state, Utah, is making plans to offer "virtual vouchers" for high school students to take a wide range of digital classes.

Given what I know about the promise of educational technology, and also because I'm hopeful by nature, I'm looking at these trends optimistically. It's entirely possible that the painful recession still lingering as I write could be fortuitous for education, if it serves to accelerate the adoption of new digital technologies, combined with the new complex-systems view of learning, that will help each and every student get more engaged in learning.

As I've mentioned, however, there's a big potential downside to this exciting moment, with the risk that we'll do worse than merely squander our once-in-a-lifetime opportunity. What worries me the most, as I watch the rush to digitize classrooms, is not so much the lure of the vast profits to be made (indeed, I think profit, free-markets, and competition will be key for genuine progress), but rather the nature of some of the businesses pursuing them.

Utah's leading online educational content provider, for instance, is a Virginia-based for-profit firm called K12, established in 1999 and already claiming to be the biggest company in its field. Its founding CEO, Ron Packard, is a former mergers and acquisitions officer at Goldman Sachs, while a co-owner is the former junk bond billionaire and securities fraud convict Michael Milken.

These recent investments reflect the obvious: that educational technology is a potentially high-profit pursuit. Still, there are no shortcuts when it comes to genuine learning. As much as we all love to believe in simple answers, I urge you to keep in mind that technology, in and out of the classroom, is no more than a tool. It's not by any means the solution to our problems, which are wide-ranging and complex. We still have a lot to learn, and if we end up chasing short-term profits—and even short-term test-score improvements—at this point, we'll lose our unique opportunity for a genuine learning revolution.

I worry about losing that revolution, in particular, when I hear how private companies have been increasing their influence in schools, both through the rapid increase in charters and the newer push for online content, at a time when the influence of the teacher—by far the most important determinant of educational outcomes—has been dangerously weakened. That's why, much as I admire the achievements of programs such as San Jose's Rocketship, I was concerned to hear that the school has been cutting costs by hiring people without teaching certificates to monitor the computerized learning. I sincerely doubt that a high-quality education can be had without a quality teacher.

Left unchecked, these sorts of trends could indeed lead to the nightmare vision that Ravitch suggests, of students studying "in isolation, sitting in their basements at home, not having to learn how to deal with people, how to cope with cliques, how to work out problems with other children, how to function in a group."

The good news, however, is that there are plenty of people—and I proudly count myself among them—working hard to prevent this education doomsday and make sure that technology actually improves life in the classroom, both for students and teachers. We believe that the true potential of these new technologies comes not in the opportunity to cut back on teachers' time (and pay) but to free them up for the kind of high-impact activities they love most and do best. For example, technological innovations are already sparing some teachers hours of rote tasks, such as taking attendance, and relieving them of the mindless crowd management duties that now take up so much of their days. In this way, technology becomes an extension, not a substitute, for human abilities and relationships.

There are many examples of this smarter, innovative approach to technology in progress throughout the nation. Many of the schools that I have in mind are known as "hybrids," which manage to combine high-tech and up-to-date teaching approaches sometimes referred to as "high touch."

Hybrid Havens

The school that may best exemplify this ideal is San Diego's High Tech High, the public charter school system where principal Larry Rosenstock has set clear limits on his schools' digital content. For example, High Tech High schools use the widely acclaimed online Rosetta Stone programs to study foreign languages, while some also receive limited online tutoring in math. But Rosenstock recently rejected a proposal to bring students to campus just one day a week, with the other four days spent at home online, arguing that he wants to keep the emphasis on high-quality human relationships.

Luckily, hybrid models like High Tech High are catching on—again, not just at charter or private schools but at many public schools as well. Rosenstock's own charter, at this writing, was expanding to include eleven schools, while also dedicating substantial resources to replicating its success in other districts throughout the country.

Another pathbreaking project, the national Big Picture Learning organization, has had striking success with its high-tech and high-touch approach, particularly with so-called at-risk students, ever since its first school, the Metropolitan Regional Career and Technical Center (the "Met"), opened in 1996 in Rhode Island. Currently, more than seventy Big Picture public and charter schools are active in fourteen states, with more than nine thousand students. While the schools take advantage of new technologies, their main emphasis is on the emotional component of learning, with classwork designed to address the interests and goals of each student, in order to build motivation. Class sizes are small, while each student is assigned to a mentor who guides them through real-world-focused internships. With considerable financial backing from the Bill & Melinda Gates Foundation, the Big Picture schools have racked up stunning records, with on-time graduation rates on average topping 90 percent and a college acceptance rate of 95 percent.

Make no mistake: I consider myself an evangelist for much

more rather than less high-tech tools in the classroom, as long as we make sure that the systems genuinely improve the classroom experience, as demonstrated so well at High Tech High and the Big Picture schools. Among other things, this means we must remain alert to the impact that all curricula, digital or not, is having on students' emotions—including their sense of achievement and mastery, so important in driving their motivation to learn.

Disruptive, in a Good Way

As Harvard Business School professor Clayton Christensen has so brilliantly pointed out in his book *Disrupting Class*, digital content has become a "disruptive" force in education, challenging antiquated strategies that have been marginalizing far too many children over the past two centuries. As I've suggested above, the best way this can happen is if technology supports instead of attempts to replace the talented teaching in evidence at places like High Tech High and Big Picture Learning.

As I've collaborated over the past several years with educators, academics, and nonprofit and for-profit groups engaged in the education revolution, I've zeroed in on what I see as three keys to the future success of this hybrid model. Specifically, it will depend on: an understanding of variability, improvements in the way we test, and a democratic approach to content. Let's take them one by one.

Since I've already talked your ear off about **variability** all through this book, I'll keep this section short. The bottom line: Parents and teachers should assume tremendous variability in how children learn and behave, owing both to inborn influences and the powerful role of context. And it's entirely fair to expect that new digital learning technologies be capable of actually supporting these differences. Decade after decade, textbook publishers have been able to get by with creating material for the "average" student, who, as we now know, has never existed. Yet as I've described in the case of the science notebook, recent innovations offer huge new potential for more flexibility in this regard. We already have both the scientific knowledge and technologies to make this breakthrough in a cost-effective way—and we simply can't afford to let this opportunity pass us by.

That's good news for you, and for literally millions of kids— especially if we can build on the advances we've made to counter the forces of mediocrity that are embodied, most dramatically, in the pervasive practice of **standardized tests**. These tests have become wildly unpopular in recent years, for good reasons. They were never designed to provide the real-time feedback that students need to learn effectively; instead, they were meant to rank and sort.

Under the banner of "accountability," they force teachers to race through material and favor superficial insights rather than genuine engagement and deep knowledge. They encourage a teaching-to-the-norm approach that alienates many students. And if all that weren't enough, research has shown the tests truly do not measure how well most students are learning. Given what we know today about students' variability when it comes to learning, I believe that there is no justification to continue the practice of standardized testing.

Now, testing per se isn't so bad—quite the contrary. Scientists have found that being provided with frequent and relevant feedback is a remarkably effective way to learn. Students need to know when they're making progress, and reviewing under some pressure is helpful, provided the assessment is focused on measuring learning, not ranking students. As long as it's done right, such testing offers a classic example of a positive feedback loop.

Here again, digital technology offers the promise of something better. What's coming your way soon—under the name of "learning analytics"—are assessment and feedback systems that can monitor and evaluate not just the student, but the curriculum itself. Students will be able to "talk back" to the material, noting when they don't understand it. The curriculum authors will get rapid streams of feedback alerting them when they need to modify the material. I'm excited by this progress, which makes so much more sense than today's practice of assuming that any student's failure to learn is purely the student's fault. Instead, by embedding these new feedback loops in the curriculum, the instruction method will constantly improve as the students also get smarter.

It's still early days for this system, and it's far from perfect, but I think that it is an important step toward genuine personalization, and one bound to be widely replicated. Now, how can we guarantee that the digital tide sweeping through U.S. classrooms actually improves learning for as many students as possible? Ideally, as this revolution unfolds, it will resemble the path of the Internet itself, in which open-source **democracy** has fostered an amazing amount of creativity. In this way, America's best teachers, or even people who might never have thought of themselves as teachers, can become the next generation's teaching "rock stars" by devising innovative ways to explain and demonstrate material.

Consider the disruptive work of Salman Khan, a former Boston hedge fund analyst and the son of immigrants from India and what is now Bangladesh. Several years ago, when Kahn was still in his late twenties, his seventh-grade cousin in New Orleans asked him for help with her math homework. Using a notepad software program, he tutored her over the Internet on how to convert kilograms to pounds, and in the process discovered his calling. He subsequently launched the nonprofit Khan Academy, originally headquartered in his converted closet, and which to date has produced more than three thousand free educational videos on topics ranging from trigonometry to banking to biology. (It also offers free, comprehensive preparation for the SAT.) At last count, Khan's site was getting millions of visits every day, while Bill Gates has praised it as "a glimpse of the future of education." Google has given Khan $2 million, citing the academy as one of several projects that "would help the world most."

It's a vivid measure of the mounting frustration with conventional education that Khan has so quickly achieved such acclaim with so simple a formula. His videos, each just a few minutes long, follow a Spartan format, with Khan's energetic, disembodied voice giving instructions as a piece of chalk draws diagrams on a blackboard. The key, Khan explains, is that viewers can speed him up when they get bored or slow him down when they need to review the material, without worrying about looking impatient or stupid—making the Khan Academy the closest thing yet to Tim Blair's dream of a device that can remotely control your teacher.

Khan's approach sends a loud warning signal to stuck-in-their-ways, brick-and-mortar schools. While, as critics have pointed out, his "academy" is really something less than that—more like educational booster shots—the basic idea is so good that it's bound to spread quickly, allowing the most skillful teachers a much wider audience. That's why I love what Khan has done so far, while I'm even more excited to think of it as barely scratching the surface of what's possible.

Expert Learners

I hope that by now you can appreciate both the breadth and speed of the learning revolution on its way. Still, that doesn't mean you can afford to sit back and wait for it. There is plenty for you to do to help prepare your child for the future. The job starts by remembering the famous exhortation on the walls of the Temple of Apollo at Delphi in ancient Greece. *Know thyself.*

The motto is a helpful reminder for anyone, but essential for challenging kids like I was, and their parents, who recognize that homes are just as powerful learning environment as schools. Knowing yourself—and your child—as I've suggested all through this book, means understanding how you operate as part of a complex system—how different environments help or hinder your behavior, and what kinds of supports and resources you need to ask for to succeed in those environments that aren't a good fit. This is how you start to gain control, to make the most of your particular strengths and weaknesses, and move on to achieve your goals. More specifically, this is how you can learn to navigate the new digital learning environments that are going to be offering you unprecedented flexibility and options. Scientists can build the best learning environments in the world, yet people are still going to have to work out how to make the most of them, a task that involves becoming expert learners.

I'm confident that lots of kids will step up to this challenge. What keeps me hopeful about the learning revolution under way is that today's battles aren't just being fought only by big companies like Google and Apple, or even by Harvard scientists. The most energetic rebels are students themselves, who in just the past few decades have recognized their inalienable rights—to life, liberty, and the pursuit of a quality education, without having to get tortured by boredom in the process.

Tim Blair, the young advocate I mentioned earlier, belongs to the advance guard. To date, Blair hasn't thrown any stink bombs, like I did back in Utah, although, as he confides, he did once take part in an aborted plot to sabotage his fifth-grade musical with fart spray. While other kids like him, who were so often misunderstood, got "sad," Blair says, he got angry. He believes he has as much of a right to be educated as "normal kids," and that, in fact, society needs his kind of out-of-the-box energy.

I agree, of course. What's more, when I consider the way kids like Tim Blair are newly aware of their right to a genuine education—and when I reflect on how kids like Dan are getting second chances in school, thanks to a new focus on variability and context—I've got reason to hope that they and millions of other square pegs are on their way to a much brighter future.

BIG IDEAS
• ▪ • ▪ • ▪ ▪ •

▪ Technologies such as digital notebooks are providing new ways to support the natural variability that students bring to the classroom, thus allowing more kids to discover their talents and reach their full potential.

▪ A combination of unprecedented pressure to cut education budgets and a strong new profit potential will make more digital learning inevitable in schools, for better or for worse.

▪ The promise of more digital learning carries the risk that bean counters will try to replace teachers with software. That would be a big mistake. Good teachers are critically important, and new digital technologies are at their best when they remove barriers that prevent those teachers from doing what *they* do best.

▪ Three features vital to the smart development of digital learning are respect for students' variability, smart testing, and democracy, by which I mean open-source authoring.

ACTION ITEMS
● ■ ● ● ● ■ ● ● ■ ● ● ● ■

- Investigate your child's school's approach to digital learning to make sure it isn't a knee-jerk cost-cutting strategy and that administrators maintain a healthy respect for human relationships.
- Encourage your son or daughter to face and understand his or her variability. In a practical sense, it's your first step to pursuing any needed accommodations in school. If you do it right, you'll be giving your child a gift that will keep on giving.

Acknowledgments

From Todd Rose and Katherine Ellison:

In writing this book, we were privileged to be able to rely on an extraordinary complex system of talented supporters and positive feedback loops. We owe a large debt of gratitude to our literary agent, Michelle Tessler; editors Leslie Wells and Elisabeth Dyssegaard; and copy editor Tom Pitoniak for seeing this project through from its earliest stages. We also suspect we won the jackpot when Kerri Kolen stepped in, just before publication, to share our vision and devote her considerable talents to making sure many others did as well.

From Todd Rose:

I'm grateful to so many people in the course of my life who've helped me to understand myself, fall in love with learning, and, most recently, produce this book. I thank Katherine Ellison for her dedication and hard work and especially for encouraging me to be as honest as possible when it came to discussing the most difficult and painful parts of my story.

As I recall the many generous mentors who have helped me not only survive but thrive in school, I'm also indebted to Bill McVaugh, Eric Amsel, Julianne Arbuckle, and, above all, Kurt Fischer for introducing me to complex systems, for being such a great scientist and an even better human being, and for teaching me to become the best square peg I could possibly be. I also owe special thanks to several colleagues who directly and indirectly contributed their time and ideas, including: David Rose, Anne Meyer, Gabrielle Rappolt-Schlichtmann, and David Gordon, as well as Walter Haas, Parisa Rouhani, and Andrew McCollum.

My largest debt of gratitude is to my mother and father, Lyda and Larry Rose; my grandma Ruth Burton; and my wife, Kaylin, and two sons, Austin and Nathan, not only for reading and commenting on various drafts of the book, but for providing my life's story with the happiest of endings.

From Katherine Ellison:

I met Todd Rose at a difficult time.

My eldest son, then twelve years old, was struggling in school and at home, and like millions of other parents in this predicament, I was scrambling for ideas about how to help him. Luckily for me, that's when I happened to see a video featuring Todd's inspiring comeback story. I looked him up at Harvard, and we talked each other's ears off. In the intervening years, I've relied repeatedly on Todd's unique ability to so clearly remember what it was like to be a deeply misunderstood kid at the mercy of an archaic school system, on his practical ideas for how to help, and more than anything else on his faith that this, too, will pass.

Today, Todd and I share the hope that our book can help other parents in similar ways, while also speeding the day when American schools become places that make our children more, not less, emotionally sound and that prize and nurture kids' energy and creativity, troublesome as it so often can be.

All this is to explain why I'm grateful first to Todd for the opportunity to collaborate on this project, and, next, to his parents, Lyda and Larry, for their rare honesty and good will. Once again, I also thank my own circle of family and friends for all the laughs, love, and wisdom. This includes the North 24th Writers: Allison Bartlett, Leslie Crawford, Frances Dinkelspiel, Sharon Epel, Susan Freinkel, Katherine Neilan, Lisa Okuhn, Julia Flynn Siler, and Jill Storey, as well as Katy Butler, Nancy Boughey, Pauline Craig, Emily Goldfarb, and Jill Wolfson; and never least, Bernice, Ellis, David, and James Ellison; Jean Milofsky; and Jack, Joseph, and Joshua Epstein.

Notes

Prologue

1   "The difficulty lies": John Maynard Keynes, *The General Theory of Employment, Interest and Money* (Harcourt, Brace and Company, 1936).

1   smell of burning sulfur: See, for fun, Daniel Engber, "The Smell of Hell: Does Satan reek of rotten eggs?," *Slate*, September 22, 2006, http://www.slate.com/id/2150170.

7   set off a tornado in Texas: Y. Udea, "Explosion of strange attractors exhibited by Duffing's equation," International Conference on Nonlinear Dynamics, New York, December 17–21, 1979, New York Academy of Sciences, *Annals*, vol. 357, December 26, 1980, pp. 422–34.

14   seven thousand students a day: See, for example, statement by the White House, March 1, 2010, "President Obama Announces Steps to Reduce Dropout Rate and Prepare Students for College and Careers."

14   we've all heard legends: While Albert Einstein is frequently cited as belonging to this group of successful high school dropouts, the circumstances of his leaving high school in fact didn't fit

the normal pattern of failing grades and boredom. Two modern biographies confirm that he left his German high school early, chiefly in order to rejoin his parents, who had moved to Italy.

15 more than 80 percent of U.S. prison inmates: James E. Ysseldyke, Bob Algozzine, and Martha L. Thurlow, *Critical Issues in Special Education* (Boston: Houghton Mifflin, 1992).

15 $240 billion a year: National Dropout Prevention Network, as cited by C. A. Winter, "Learning disabilities, crime, delinquency, and special education placement," *Adolescence,* Summer 1997; http://findarticles.com/p/articles/mi_m2248/is_n126_v32/ai _19619426/pg_2/.

15 5 percent of all high school dropouts are intellectually gifted: http: //www.all4ed.org/files/archive/publications/HighCost.pdf. The lowest-achieving 25 percent of students are twenty times more likely to drop out of high school than students in the highest achievement quartile. See Anthony P. Carnevale, "Help wanted . . . College required," Educational Testing Service, Office of Public Leadership, Washington, D.C. See also Michael S. Matthews, "Gifted Learners Who Drop Out: Prevalence and Prevention," in *International Handbook on Giftedness*, Springer Science + Business Media, 2009, DOI10.1007/978-1-4010-6162 -2-24.

16 originated in early-nineteenth-century Prussia: Henry Geitz, Jurgen Heideking, and Jurgen Herbst, eds., *German Influences on Education in the United States to 1917* (New York: Cambridge University Press, 1995).

17 as many as 36 percent will drop out: Sam Goldstein and Anne Teeter-Ellison, *Clinician's Guide to Adult ADHD: Assessment and Intervention* (San Diego: Academic Press, 2002).

17 half of all U.S. prison inmates: Clyde A. Winters, "Learning disabilities, crime, delinquency, and special education placement," *Adolescence,* summer 1997, cited at http://findarticles.com/p /articles/mi_m2248/is_n126_v32/ai_19619426.

Chapter 1

21 Not once throughout my first two years: Susan Shur-Fen Gau and Huey-Ling Chiang, "Sleep Problems and Disorders among Adolescents with Persistent and Subthreshold Attention-deficit/Hyperactivity Disorders," *Sleep*, May 1, 2009.

25 "the Rosenthal effect": See, for instance, Robert Rosenthal and Lenore Jacobson, "Teachers' expectancies: Determinates of pupils' IQ gains," *Psychological Reports* 19, no. 115–18 (1966); Robert Rosenthal and Lenore Jacobson, *Pygmalion in the Classroom: Teacher Expectations and Pupils' Intellectual Development* (New York: Holt, Rinehart & Winston, 1968).

Chapter 2:

43 my mom's sister, Betty: This is an alias.

45 "working" memory: On the relationship to academic achievement, see R. G. Alloway, "Investigating the predictive roles of working memory and IQ in academic attainment," *Journal of Experimental Child Psychology* 106 (2010): 20–29.

47 "learned helplessness": For multiple articles, see http://www.ppc .sas.upenn.edu/lh.htm.

51 "an underestimated force in education": Video of Wilhelm at http: //wn.com/Jeffrey_Wilhelm_on_Is_school_boring.

51 Thom Hartmann: http://en.wikipedia.org/wiki/Thom Hartmann.

52 that didn't stop me from hating the Ritalin: Compliance is a serious problem in ADHD medications. San Francisco–area pediatrician Peter Levine, a leader in ADHD treatment for Kaiser Permanente, says children stay on the meds an average of only eighteen months.

53 My mother never tried to get my school to pay: By federal law, schools are supposed to provide thorough diagnostic testing when there is evidence that a child might have a learning disorder.

56   children with major disabilities: http://febp.newamerica.net/back
      ground-analysis/individuals-disabilities-education-act-over-
      view.

60   ineffective at best: One of my favorite articles on the bad effects of
      corporal punishment is this one, by psychologist Alan E. Kaz-
      din, past president of the American Psychological Association:
      http://www.slate.com/id/2200450.

Chapter 3

65   "what you see and hear depends": The quote is from *The Magician's
      Nephew*, written between 1949 and 1954. The first study of
      MRI brain scans on humans was published in 1977.

66   to shoo away loitering teens: http://www.huffingtonpost.com/2008
      /04/23/high-pitch-only-teens-can_n_98304.html.

67   studying a group of talented astrophysicists: For a review of the
      original theory, see: M. H. Schneps, T. L. Rose, and K. W.
      Fischer, "Visual Learning and the Brain: Implications for Dys-
      lexia," *Journal of Mind, Brain, and Education* 1, no. 3 (2007).

70   "the wick in the candle of learning": M. J. Kang et al., "The wick in
      the candle of learning: Epistemic curiosity activates reward cir-
      cuitry and enhances memory," *Psychological Science* 20 (2009):
      963–73.

72   wrong about the broader question: An interesting look at just this
      broader question is Todd Barrett Kashdan and Mantak Yuen,
      "Whether highly curious students thrive academically depends
      on perceptions about the school learning environment: A study
      of Hong Kong adolescents," published online, October 23, 2007,
      Springer Science + Business Media.

74   In 2008, Dan Eisenberg: Eisenberg was the lead author on a study
      involving collaboration with Ben Campbell, an evolutionary
      anthropologist at the University of Wisconsin at Milwaukee:
      http://informsciencenetwork.com/anthropology/latest-hyper
      activity-evolve-survival-aid-nomads-2350866a; http://www.north

western.edu/newscenter/stories/2008/06/ariaaltribe.html;
http://www.biomedcentral.com/1471-2148/8/173/abstract; and
interviews by phone and e-mail with Dan Eisenberg, winter
2010.

76 "We were working": There's a striking parallel here with Buddhist
teachings, which advise that it takes "skillful means" to teach
wisdom to people who vary so much in their capacity to understand. The same truth, said the Buddha, may be understood
through no less than eighty-four thousand "Dharma doors":
http://www.buddhism.org/Sutras/3.

78 influencing policy from the federal level on down: In collaboration with Harvard Law School, Boston College, and others,
CAST has led a federally funded project that has culminated
in the writing of the first-ever National Instructional Materials Accessibility Standard, or NIMAS. NIMAS, which has the
force of federal education law, requires publishers to develop
textbooks and other learning materials in a flexible digital format so they can be quickly transformed from a single source
file into Braille, e-text, human-voice narration, and other accessible formats.

79 Ben Foss: Learn about the advocacy group Foss created and watch
his terrific video about dyslexia at http://www.headstrongnation
.org/; http://www.ldonline.org/firstperson/Benjamin_Foss.

79 Stutts had sued: http://law.justia.com/cases/federal/appellate-courts
/F2/694/666/116830.

80 "for the lazy and infirm": "Intel Reader reads books to the lazy and
infirm (video)," posted by Vlad Savov, November 10, 2009,
Engadget.com: http://www.engadget.com/2009/11/10/intel-reader
-reads-books-to-the-lazy-and-infirm-video.

Chapter 4

90 an estimated 13 million students: http://www.telegraph.co.uk/news
/worldnews/barackobama/8375091/Barack-Obama-shares
-childhood-tales-at-bullying-conference.html.

91   President Barack Obama presided: http://www.cnn.com/2011/POL
      ITICS/03/10/obama.bullying/index.html. The White House also
      launched a website, www.Stopbullying.gov.

91   "dispel the myth": Obama backed up his words with a pledge to
      include $132 million in the 2012 budget to combat violence and
      the bullying of children, providing grants to state and local gov-
      ernments under the Education Department's Successful, Safe,
      and Healthy Students program.

91   a great deal of recent research: http://www.bullyingstatistics.org/con
      tent/bullying-statistics-2009.html; http://www.pascack.k12.nj.us
      /70271919141818/lib/70271919141818/Bullying_Statistics.htm;
      http://students.com.miami.edu/netreporting/?page_id=1269.

91   where bullying is most common: "Bullying Behaviors Among US
      Youth: Prevalence and Association With Psychosocial Adjust-
      ment," Tonja R. Nansel, Ph.D., *The Journal of the American Med-
      ical Association* 285 (2001): 2094–2100.

91   than if I'd been a girl: "Predictors of Bullying and Victimization in
      Childhood and Adolescence: A Meta-analytic Investigation,"
      Clayton R. Cook, et al., *School Psychology Quarterly*, 25, no. 2
      (2010): 65–83 (1045–3830).

91   as a boy with learning struggles: See this blog by Marlene Snyder,
      Ph.D., Understanding Bullying and Its Impact on Kids With
      Learning Disabilities or AD/HD, http://www.greatschools.org
      /special-education/health/823-understanding-bullying-and-its
      -impact-on-kids-with-learning-disabilities-or-ad-hd.gs.

91   About one in five victims: S. M. Swearer and B. J. Doll, "Bullying
      in schools: An ecological framework," *Journal of Emotional
      Abuse* 2 (2001): 7–23.

92   "I wake up and my stomach": Student Advisors for Education, *Read
      This When You Can: Stories and Essays by SAFE Voices* (San Fran-
      cisco: Parents Education Network, 2008).

92   both types of pain activate: Ethan Kross, et al., "Social rejection
      shares somatosensory representations with physical pain," *Pro-
      ceedings of the National Academy of Sciences* (2011).

93 "For 99 percent of the beasts": http://www.dana.org/news/cerebrum /detail.aspx?id=638.

93 bullying dumbs you down: Scientists hypothesize that the stress of being bullied depresses immune functioning through the action of the stress hormone cortisol. See, for instance, Emily Anthes, "Inside the Bullied Brain: The Alarming Neuroscience of Taunting," *Boston Globe*, Nov. 28, 2010.

94 shoot down as far as the second percentile: http://psycnet.apa.org /psycinfo/2007-06470-007. Learning is simply not a priority: Research that should come as no surprise has found that students involved in bullying and victimization are less academically engaged. See, for instance, "The Association of Bullying and Victimization with Middle School Adjustment," Tonja R. Nansel, et al, *Journal of Applied School Psychology*, 19, no. 2 (2003). Other research has demonstrated that, over the long term, the cortisol response can impair the brain's prefrontal cortex, a key tool in self-control. A child who perceives himself as under threat for a long time will typically become hypervigilant, emotionally reactive, defensive, and quick to anger.

94 a diagnosis of oppositional defiant disorder: See, for example, http: //aacap.org/page.ww?name=Children+with+Oppositional+Defi ant+Disorder&section=Facts+for+Families.

96 I put a big smiley face on my miserable life: The story of my visit to Goldstein highlights one of the biggest limitations of the whole clinical psychology enterprise—the significant possibility that the patient (particularly a disgruntled adolescent patient) isn't telling the truth. There was really no chance that I was going to open up to a guy I'd never met, whom I'd been taken to see for the express purpose (at least in my opinion at the time) of discovering what was wrong with me. At the time, I assumed Goldstein's report would be available to anyone who wanted to see it, so why shouldn't I have guarded my privacy?

98 someone had to detach and deescalate: Lyda's parenting decision is supported by research showing that kids in conflict with mothers maintain higher levels of cortisol through the school day. See G. Rappolt-Schlichtmann et al., "Poverty, Relationship

Conflict, and the Regulation of Cortisol in Small and Large Group Contexts at Child Care," *Mind, Brain, and Education* 3 (2009): 131–42.

Chapter 5

109 "Opposite Todd": The *Seinfeld* episode in fact aired in 1994, one year before I figured out this approach on my own, but I credit the show for the brand name.

120 psychologist Carol Dweck: See Dweck's website: http://mindseton line.com/.

Chapter 6

132 Gabrielle Rappolt-Schlichtmann: Here is Rappolt-Schlichtmann's profile, at CAST: http://www.cast.org/about/staff/grappolt-schli chtmann.html.

132 even if their "rational" brain networks: See, for example, http://www -bcf.usc.edu/~immordin/papers/Immordino-Yang+Damasio _2007_RelevanceofNeurotoEdu.pdf.

134 their resources are at least roughly equal to the demands: Blasco-vich and Tomaka updated their work most recently in 2008: J. Blascovich, "Challenge and Threat," in A. J. Elliot, ed., *Hand-book of Approach and Avoidance Motivation* (New York: Erl-baum, 2008), pp. 431–46. This description is also based with Ellison's phone interview with Blascovich, May 27, 2011.

136 enough to make anyone more confident: Interestingly, the psycholo-gist Sian Beilock has found that too *much* audience support can be counterproductive for sports teams. Home teams may be at a major disadvantage during playoffs or championship games be-cause the cheering raises the pressure to perform, and leads to players becoming anxious. http://discovermagazine.com/2010/the -brain-2/06-science-reveals-how-not-to-choke-under-pressure.

137 African-American students to reaffirm their values: Gerardo Ramirez and Sian L. Beilock, "Writing about Testing Worries Boosts Exam

Performance in the Classroom," *Science,* vol. 331, January 14, 2011.

137 The "stereotype threat" research: See for instance, this interview with one of the field's founders, Stanford University professor Claude Steele: http://www.pbs.org/wgbh/pages/frontline/shows /sats/interviews/steele.html.

138 decreased bullying by up to 23 percent: See, for instance, Catherine P. Bradshaw and Tracy E. Waasdorp, "Effective Strategies in Combating Bullying," Johns Hopkins Center for the Prevention of Youth Violence, Johns Hopkins Bloomberg School of Public Health.

138 Olweus Bullying Prevention Program: D. Olweus, "The Olweus Bullying Prevention Programme: Design and implementation issues and a new national initiative in Norway," in P. K. Smith, D. Pepler, and K. Rigby, eds., *Bullying in Schools: How Successful Can Interventions Be?* (Cambridge, UK: Cambridge University Press, 2004), pp. 13–36. The program has been touted by experts including the American Academy of Pediatrics. See http://www.clemson.edu/olweus/aap.pdf.

139 David Farrington and Maria Ttofi: David P. Farrington and Maria M. Ttofi, *School-based Programs to Reduce Bullying and Victimization,* Campbell Systematic Reviews (Oslo: Campbell Collaboration, 2009).

139 "Just Say No": In 2006, a ten-year study by the American Psychological Association, involving one thousand D.A.R.E. graduates, found no measurable effects of the program. The researchers compared levels of alcohol, cigarette, marijuana, and illegal substances use before the D.A.R.E. program (when the students were in sixth grade) with the post-D.A.R.E. levels (when they were twenty years old). Although there were some measured effects shortly after the program on the attitudes of the students toward drug use, these effects did not seem to carry on long term. http://psycnet.apa.org/index.cfm?fa=buy.optionToBuy&id =1999-03346-017.

139 zero-tolerance policies: In recent years, there has been mounting concern about the prejudicial impacts of such increasingly harsh

school policies. See for example this report on a recent study of Texas schools: http://www.nytimes.com/2011/07/19/education /19discipline.html?_r=1&pagewanted=print.

140 In 2011, the first major analysis of these programs: Joseph A. Durlak et al., "The Impact of Enhancing Students' Social and Emotional Learning: A Meta-Analysis of School-Based Universal Interventions," *Child Development* 82, no. 1 (2011). See also http://www .sciencedaily.com/releases/2011/02/110204091243.htm.

141 High Tech High: http://www.newschools.org/about/news/articles /future-schools. Ellison visited High Tech High and interviewed Larry Rosenstock in March 2011.

142 "with teachers becoming": The interview with Rosenstock is available at http://dp.hightechhigh.org/~lrosenstock/prs_converge1. html.

145 they tend to excel: Several studies have found that schools that provide a positive culture and healthy challenges for students have less bullying, whereas poorly managed schools have more. See, for example, Stephen Brand et al., "Middle school improvement and reform: Development and validation of a school-level assessment of climate, cultural pluralism, and school safety," *Journal of Educational Psychology*, 95, no. 2 (Sept. 2003): 570–88.

Chapter 7

152 being kind to oneself: See, for example, http://well.blogs.nytimes .com/2011/02/28/go-easy-on-yourself-a-new-wave-of-research -urges.

152 more happy and optimistic than others: K. Neff, "The role of self-compassion in development: A healthier way to relate to oneself," *Human Development* 52 (2009): 211–14.

152 dieting to lose weight: So says a book by a Harvard colleague of mine, Jean Fain, in her book *The Self-Compassion Diet* (Boulder, CO: Sounds True, 2011).

157 Strong relationships between fathers and children: These findings and more can be found documented at www.theboysinitiative

.org (Among the most interesting of the studies on this site, published in June 2010, and involving more than a million Swedish children six to nineteen, found that both boys and girls were 54 percent more likely to be on ADHD medication if they were raised by a single parent. Fewer than half the cases could be explained by socioeconomic factors.)

161 the importance of mentors: See, for example, "Supportive Non-Parental Adults and Adolescent Psychosocial Functioning: Using Social Support as a Theoretical Framework," http://www.ncbi .nlm.nih.gov/pubmed/21384233, and Katy Butler, "The Anatomy of Resilience," *Psychotherapy Networker,* March–April 1997, http://www.katybutler.com/publications/psychnetorg/index _files/psychthernet_anatofresilience.htm.

163 federally sponsored researchers have found: See, for example, E. H. Nieweg, "Does ADHD medication stop working after 2–3 years? On the surprising but little-known follow-up of the MTA study," *Tijdschr Psychiatry* 52, no. 4 (2010): 245–54, http://www.ncbi .nlm.nih.gov/pubmed/20503165.

167 I actually enjoyed learning: Of course, there were still times when my impulsive "wit" got me into trouble. For example, on the first day of my sociology class, the professor asked everyone to stand and introduce themselves. On my turn, I stood up and said, I suppose just for fun, "Hi, I'm Todd Rose, and I'm an alcoholic." Some people laughed, others shrugged it off. But one woman, whom I'll call Nancy, looked furious. After class, she cornered me and told me that her husband was a recovering alcoholic and that had wrecked her family to the point where she was coming to school to try to start over. "What kind of person makes jokes about something like that?" she asked. I knew she was right, and felt so embarrassed that I went a bit overboard in my reaction. "Actually," I replied somberly, "I know what you are talking about. But I have been clean for almost three years. And I've found that humor allows me to get on with life in a way that taking things too seriously does not." Nancy became my best friend in that class, and if she's reading this now, I sure hope she forgives me.

Chapter 8

176 "syllabuses": http://www.merriam-webster.com/dictionary/syllabi.

184 suppressing unwelcome bits of reality: This explanation, and the story of Kevin Dunbar's research, comes from a fascinating story in *Wired* magazine: http://www.wired.com/magazine/2009/12/fail _accept_defeat/

187 the immediate aftermath of any error: Malcolm Gladwell has written a particularly insightful story illustrating the value of thwarting the habit of denial sufficiently to learn from one's mistakes. It's at http://www.gladwell.com/1999/1999_08_02_a_genius.htm.

187 strategy known as reframing: A nice overview is at http://www.psy chologytoday.com/blog/eyes-the-brain/201104/seeing-yourself -differently-through-reframing.

Epilogue

198 science notebook: The ungainly early name for the notebook proto-type is the SNUDLE. The Science Notebook team has been headed by CAST scientist Gabrielle Rappolt-Schlichtmann and created with financing from the U.S. Department of Education. You can find out more about the notebook at http://www.cast .org/research/projects/snudl.html. Of course, the notebook is just one of a large number of innovative classroom technologies starting to come into use. I'm also excited about innovations such as the new smart-pen system developed by a company called LiveScribe, http://www.livescribe.com/en-us/, which si-multaneously takes notes and records audio content, with an option by which you can tap on a note and hear all that was said that you forgot to write down.

199 "unimpeded excellence": See David George Ritchie, *Natural Rights: A Criticism of Some Political and Ethical Conceptions* (New York: Macmillan, 1895), available at http://books.google.com/books?id =o0OFAAAAMAAJ&pg=PA274&lpg=PA274&dq=happiness+ unimpeded+excellence&source=bl&ots=QvNQkLhDeO& sig=SKewNVJzORSne9_6FRhm8SXhaZw&hl=en&ei=ritVTqvr

OMfjiALpi_ngDA&sa=X&oi=book_result&ct=result&res
num=6&ved=0CDYQ6AEwBQ#v=onepage&q=happiness
%20unimpeded%20excellence&f=false.

203 Diane Ravitch: Ravitch is the author of, among other works, *The
Death and Life of the Great American School System: How Testing
and Choice are Undermining Education.* Her quote comes from
a radio interview with Democracy Now, http://vimeo.com
/28201779. The transcript is available at http://www.alternet.org
/news/152182/%22poverty_is_the_problem%22_with_our_pub
lic_schools,_not_teachers%27_unions?page=5.

203 In the decade beginning with the year 2000: Heather Staker et al.,
"The Rise of K–12 Blended Learning Profiles of Emerging
Models," Innosite Institute, May 2011.

203 At this writing, more than half a million: http://www.cnbc.com/id
/44255406/Online_Grade_Schools_Becoming_a_Popular_Al
ternative. Furthermore, nationwide, an estimated 1.03 million
students at the K–12 level took an online course in 2007–2008,
up 47 percent from two years earlier, according to the Sloan
Consortium, an advocacy group for online education.

204 thousands of U.S. schools: See also this *New York Times* story:
http://www.nytimes.com/2011/04/06/education/06online.html.
A related development, by the way, is that some private schools,
at this writing, have been using new memory-training programs
to help their students sharpen their minds. The two leading
companies in this burgeoning new field are Cogmed and Lumosity, both offering programs developed by cognitive scientists.
See: http://www.cogmed.com and http://www.lumosity.com. Of
the two, Cogmed has an impressive number of supportive studies, suggesting the program can help kids with working memory
deficits. Cogmed is substantially more rigorous and also more
expensive than Lumosity, requiring a coach and costing about
$1,500.

204 School of One: http://www.theatlantic.com/magazine/archive/2010
/07/the-littlest-schoolhouse/8132/07/21/2009.

205 Rocketship Education: See: http://newlearningonline.com/2011/05
/11/series-focuses-on-rocketships-success.

205   DSST: For more background, see the editorial in the *Denver Post*: http://www.denverpost.com/opinion/ci_18471934.

205   close to half of all students: http://www.thefiscaltimes.com/Arti cles/2010/10/28/High-College-Dropout-Rate-Threatens-US -Growth.aspx#.

205   America's rapidly declining rate of college grads: The United States in recent years has dropped from first to ninth place in the world in college graduates. See this interview with U.S. educa- tion secretary Arne Duncan: http://marketplace.publicradio.org /display/web/2011/04/05/am-arne-duncan-on-the-future-of-ed ucation-in-the-us.

206   Schwarzenegger's switch: http://www.clrn.org/fdti/; http://arstech nica.com/tech-policy/news/2009/06/open-source-digital -textbooks-coming-to-california-schools.ars; http://www.csmon itor.com/USA/2009/0611/p02s14-usgn.html; http://www.con vergemag.com/edtech/Digital-Textbook-Run-Down.html.

207   In 2010, the foundation partnered: http://www.prnewswire.com /news-releases/nasa-teams-with-ck-12-foundation-on-physics -flexbook-103465599.html.

207   Even my own home state, Utah: Here's a description of the Utah Online Education project by one of its promoters: http://www .huffingtonpost.com/tom-vander-ark/utah-poised-to-lead-in-on _b_822298.html. On the other hand, a more critical report called this venture "the full employment act for online (for-profit) edu- cation providers serving high school students": http://utahgravy train.wordpress.com/2011/03/08/howard-stephenson-and-pces -judi-clark-pushing-the-vouchers-you-cant-refuse.

207   firm called K12: http://www.k12.com/; http://kpk12.com/blog/2011 /04/s-b-65-poised-to-change-online-learning-in-utah/.

208   the school has been cutting costs: http://educationnext.org/future -schools.

208   the nightmare vision that Ravitch suggests: http://www.business week.com/magazine/content/11_24/b4232076996440.htm. This might be a good opportunity to address another common worry about more computers in classrooms—along the lines

that they will be an impossible distraction for students. For instance, a 2009 Stanford University study showed that students who regularly multitasked with technology were more easily distracted—not just in the moment but long after they put their devices aside. With this peril in mind, several universities at this writing have been banning laptops in some classes, after professors complained that students were shopping for shoes and socializing through Facebook and Twitter rather than joining in discussions of the material. See, for example, http://articles.boston.com/2011-04-24/news/29469460_1_mit-social-networking-laptops. I certainly recognize that distraction is a danger that must be addressed, but don't think the answer is banning laptops altogether.

209 "high touch": The expression "high-tech and high touch" has been used in several contexts, including as the title of this book: http://www.amazon.com/High-Tech-Touch-Technology-Meaning/dp/0767903838.

210 Rosenstock recently rejected: Rosenstock talked with Katherine Ellison in San Diego in March 2011. He also discussed his wariness about increasing high-tech in this interview with New-Schools: http://www.newschools.org/news/future-schools.

210 Big Picture Learning: http://www.bigpicture.org/big-picture-history.

213 being provided with frequent and relevant feedback: A study supporting this idea made big news in January 2011: http://www.sciencemag.org/content/early/2011/01/19/science.1199327.abstract. See also http://www.nytimes.com/2011/01/21/science/21memory.html.

214 Salman Khan: http://www.npr.org/templates/story/story.php?storyId=121978193; http://blogs.forbes.com/bruceupbin/2010/10/28/khan-academy-a-name-you-need-to-know-in-2011/; http://www.npr.org/templates/story/story.php?storyId=121978193.

Bibliography

Allen, David. *Getting Things Done: The Art of Stress-Free Productivity*. New York: Penguin Books, 2001.

Barkley, Russell. *Taking Charge of ADHD*. New York: Guilford Press, 2000.

Beilock, Sian. *Choke: What the Secrets of the Brain Reveal About Getting It Right When You Have To*. New York: Free Press, 2010.

Berns, Gregory. *Iconoclast: A Neuroscientist Reveals How to Think Differently*. Boston: Harvard Business Press, 2010.

Branden, Nathaniel. *The Six Pillars of Self-Esteem*. New York: Bantam Books, 1995.

Christensen, Clayton, Curtis Johnson, and Michael Horn. *Disrupting Class: How Disruptive Innovation Will Change the Way the World Learns*. New York: McGraw-Hill, 2008.

Clark, Andy. *Supersizing the Mind: Embodiment, Action, and Cognitive Extension*. New York: Oxford University Press, 2010.

Dweck, Carol. *Mindset: The New Psychology of Success*. New York: Ballantine Books, 2007.

Gardner, Howard. *Extraordinary Minds: Portraits of 4 Exceptional Individuals and an Examination of Our Own Extraordinariness*. New York: Basic Books, 1998.

Gilbert, Daniel. *Stumbling on Happiness*. New York: Knopf, 2006.

Gladwell, Malcolm. *Outliers: The Story of Success*. Boston: Back Bay Books, 2011.

————. *The Tipping Point: How Little Things Can Make a Big Difference.* Boston: Back Bay Books, 2002.

Gleick, James. *Chaos: Making a New Science.* New York: Penguin Books, 2008.

Goldberg, Elkhonon. *The New Executive Brain: Frontal Lobes in a Complex World.* New York: Oxford University Press, 2009.

Klingberg, Torkel. *The Overflowing Brain: Information Overload and the Limits of Working Memory.* New York: Oxford Press, 2008.

Lehrer, Jonah. *How We Decide.* Boston: Mariner Books, 2010.

Meadows, Donella. *Thinking in Systems: A Primer.* Edited by Diana Wright. White River Junction, VT: Chelsea Green, 2008.

Mitchell, Melanie. *Complexity: A Guided Tour.* New York: Oxford University Press, 2009.

Mitchell, Sandra. *Unsimple Truths: Science, Complexity, and Policy.* Chicago: University of Chicago Press, 2009.

Neff, Kristin. *Self-Compassion: Stop Beating Yourself Up and Leave Insecurity Behind.* New York: William Morrow, 2011.

Nisbett, Richard. *Intelligence and How to Get It: Why Schools and Cultures Matter.* New York: Norton, 2010.

Page, Scott. *The Difference: How the Power of Diversity Creates Better Groups, Firms, Schools, and Societies.* Princeton, NJ: Princeton University Press, 2008.

Pink, Daniel, H. *Drive: The Surprising Truth About What Motivates Us.* New York: Riverhead Books, 2009.

Plomin, Robert. *Nature and Nurture: An Introduction to Human Behavioral Genetics.* Nashville, TN.: Ingram, 2004.

Ravitch, Diane. *The Death and Life of the Great American School System: How Testing and Choice Are Undermining Education.* New York: Basic Books, 2010.

Rosenthal, Robert, and Lenore Jacobson. *Pygmalion in the Classroom: Teacher Expectation and Pupils' Intellectual Development.* New York: Holt, Rinehart & Winston, 1968.

Sapolsky, Robert. *Why Zebras Don't Get Ulcers.* New York: W. H. Freeman, 2004.

Schultz, Kathryn. *Being Wrong: Adventures in the Margins of Error.* New York: Ecco, 2011.

Seligman, Martin. *Authentic Happiness.* New York: Free Press, 2002.

Smiley, Tavis. *Fail Up: 20 Lessons on Building Success from Failure.* Carlsbad, CA: SmileyBooks, 2011.

Student Advisors for Education. *Read This When You Can: Stories and Essays by SAFE Voices.* San Francisco: Parents Education Network, 2008.

Waber, Deborah. *Rethinking Learning Disabilities: Understanding Children Who Struggle in School.* White River Junction, VT: Guilford Press, 2010.